BLENDING GENRE, ALTERING STYLE

Writing Multigenre Papers

TOM ROMANO

Miami University

Boynton/Cook Publishers
HEINEMANN • Portsmouth, NH

Boynton/Cook Publishers, Inc.
A subsidiary of Reed Elsevier Inc.
361 Hanover Street
Portsmouth, NH 03801–3912
www.boyntoncook.com

Offices and agents throughout the world

Credit lines for borrowed material appear on p. 189.

Library of Congress Cataloging-in-Publication Data
Romano, Tom.
    Blending genre, altering style : writing multigenre papers / Tom Romano.
       p.   cm.
    Includes bibliographical references.
    ISBN 0-86709-478-8
      1. English language—Rhetoric—Study and teaching. 2. Creative writing—Study and teaching. 3. Report writing—Study and teaching. 4. English language—Style. 5. Literary form. I. Title.

PE1404.R635 2000
808′.042′071—dc21
                                       99-087957

Editor: Bill Varner
Production: Vicki Kasabian
Cover design: Judy Arisman
Photo of author and his great-niece, Joanna Mae Sigmon, by Dianna Sigmon
Manufacturing: Deanna Richardson

Printed in the United States of America on acid-free paper
06 05 04 03   VP   4 5 6

Dedicated to the Triumphant Lives and Buoyant Spirits
of
My Mom
Mae Romano Carnahan (1915–1999)
and
My Boyhood Friend Straight on Through
Danny Wackerly (1949–1998)
So many miss their wisdom, laughter, and
steady, benevolent light.

CONTENTS

And every one of them words rang true
and glowed like burnin' coal
pourin' off of every page
like it was written on my soul
from me to you . . .

Bob Dylan

INTRODUCTION

A second grader's mispronunciation of my last name has kept me honest as a teacher. In 1984–85 I was a graduate research assistant at Mast Way Elementary School in Lee, New Hampshire. This two-year study of children's reading and writing processes was headed by Jane Hansen and Donald Graves of the University of New Hampshire, where I was enrolled in the new doctoral program in reading and writing instruction.

And I was smug. After all, I was a new grad student in a respected program, a successful high school English teacher for thirteen years, a frequent presenter for the Ohio Writing Project, and a published author in *English Journal*. What, I wondered, could elementary school children and teachers possibly teach me? As I said, I was smug. Insufferably so. It lasted about a month.

One classroom I visited was Leslie Funkhouser's. Her second graders learned and grew in a productive reading and writing workshop. When I visited, I conferred with the children about their writing. One student, Michael, was always glad to see me, though he never pronounced my name right.

"Good morning, Mr. Morano!"

"Look what I'm writing, Mr. Morano!"

"Good-bye, Mr. Morano!"

I began to believe that there was more truth to Michael's mispronunciation than anyone realized. You see, the more I interacted with the children the more I began to squirm. My smugness was limiting my learning. I constantly underestimated them.

"Do you think your story needs a title?" I'd say to a child.

"I'm not worried about that right now. I have to get this draft done, then I'll brainstorm titles."

Or "Are you ready to publish this piece?"

"No, I need a conference with Noa first. I get good ideas when I talk to her."

I was fast becoming aware of my inadequacy as a qualitative researcher. I began to work harder to understand the children and their work. But let me tell you, my mind-set as a high school English teacher with plenty of hours logged in college literature classes, where reader response was for charlatans and literary texts had particular meanings that students couldn't possibly know . . . well, that was hard to shake.

One day as I was leaving Leslie's room after another morning of blunders, I grabbed my backpack and headed for the door.

"So long, Mr. Morano."

I sighed and thought, "I'm trying, Michael, I'm trying."

Since those days I've gotten better at learning from students. This book, in fact, would not exist were it not for the many lessons about writing multigenre papers that my students have taught me. Through the years they've done things with words on paper that have helped me better teach the students who came after them. My aim in this book is to pass on what I've learned, to help teachers at any level of education support their students in writing multigenre papers that are informative, moving, inventive, and clear.

I devoted two chapters of *Writing with Passion* (1995) to the multigenre paper. In them I described the sequence and rationale of using such papers with high school students, revealed their writing processes and attitudes, discussed our triumphs, surprises, and dilemmas. I included one entire multigenre paper by a senior.

Much has changed since I gathered the data for that book. I no longer teach high school students as I did the first seventeen years of my career. I no longer experience the emotional closeness to teenagers that comes from meeting with them every day for 180 days as they develop their literacy skills and explore writing territories only they know.

I'm in a different place now. Since 1991 I've taught only teachers and college students. Some things, however, have remained constant, even though I don't wake up sixteen-year-olds at 7:30 each morning. I'm still committed to writing and reading and teaching, still believe in the value of approximation, the necessity of good faith participation, and the blessed inevitability of growth and development. But now most of the writing samples and literacy stories I use to illustrate my teaching ideas come from teachers and college students, those I work closely with now.

In addition to learning from my students, I've also learned of multigenre possibilities from teachers, grade school through college. Often these teachers are dissatisfied with standard research papers or simply want passion restored to students' voices and visions. These teachers have taken the multigenre idea and made it their own. Their voices inform this book.

Some readers may work extensively with multigenre papers; others may be wondering what they are. Here is a definition I give to my students:

> A multigenre paper arises from research, experience, and imagination. It is not an uninterrupted, expository monolog nor a seamless narrative nor a collection of poems. A multigenre paper is composed of many genres and subgenres, each piece self-contained, making a point of its own, yet connected by theme or topic and

sometimes by language, images, and content. In addition to many genres, a multigenre paper may also contain many voices, not just the author's. The trick is to make such a paper hang together.

Definitions are helpful, but my students don't develop a clear idea of a multigenre paper until they read one. Then they begin to appreciate the multigenre paper's style, versatility, and possibilities. I've included five full multigenre papers in this book: two by college students and one each by a seventh grader, a high school sophomore, and a graduate student. I think you'll enjoy the writing—will be both moved and informed—and will find them—or parts of them—useful in sharing with your students as they and you explore multigenre writing.

In the pages ahead I'll discuss genres and subgenres, writing strategies, ideas for lessons, and the expertise of experienced multigenre teachers. In the Appendix I've listed many of their names and addresses (including e-mail), should you want to know more about how they teach multigenre at their particular grade level. I hope your journey through this book will be as fruitful for you to read as it was for me to write. It's a cinch it won't be as hard.

1 | MULTIGENRE STIRRINGS

During the summer of 1997, Susan Stires and I co-taught in the Reading and Writing Program at the University of New Hampshire. For three weeks we learned with twenty-five other teachers. One teacher in our group was Liz Olbrych from Kings Highway Elementary in Westport, Connecticut, an unpretentious, quietly articulate, and committed teacher of children.

Within days she had drawn people away from the main business of our class. Instead of merely reading and writing, many participants were reading, writing, and drawing. Liz, you see, kept a sketchbook as a vital part of her literacy. Once participants saw what she was doing, the idea spread. Soon Karen from Florida was drawing images that popped into her mind from her reading. Kris from Michigan sketched portraits of her peer group members and sent them along with her written responses to their writing. Eric from Maine began sharing his caricatures.

Art suffuses Liz Olbrych's life. The third graders in her writing workshop at Kings Highway know that picture making is a choice. Art is an integral part of the school's learning culture. It is valued for its own sake. The children also know that making pictures can be a tool to help them revise their writing. "If you entered your picture," Liz asks, "what would you see? What would you smell, hear, taste, and touch?" She invites children to "describe what you were thinking of when you drew" or to "describe the action in your picture."

Our class that summer was a safer place because of Liz's considerate, assured presence. And it was a larger, literate place, too, because of the art that she practiced in her sketchbook and shared.

On the last two mornings of the course, we met in a small, carpeted lecture room with seating on tiered levels. This gave teachers space to "perform" something that represented their accomplishment and their literate values. Most participants presented dramatic readings, usually of their own writing but sometimes of published authors; others wrote and performed skits; one teacher visually illustrated his three-week learning journey.

For the presentations we extinguished the lights in the audience and lit the small floor area. When it was Liz's turn, she came forward and placed a tape in the cassette player, then draped over a chair a large flag of Ireland, shiny with wide bands of green, white, and gold—a backdrop for her performance. She placed a transparency on the overhead projector, then turned her attention to the audience and stepped from shadow into light. Liz wore a plaid dress, denim shirt, and sandals. Her hair was pulled back off her neck, and two Claddagh earrings dangled from her ears. She snapped on the overhead and projected a watercolor she had painted a few weeks earlier.

The painting showed the view from the doorway of the cottage where her grandfather was born in Gallarus, a village in Dingle, County Kerry: a path in the foreground leading to a low stone wall by the road, a cow meandering by, a green meadow beyond the road, blue mountains in the distance. Liz had brought the painting to UNH because she wanted to write about it. Except for bits and pieces, though, she hadn't done much writing until the previous night, when talk with classmates and the pressure of the deadline compelled her to write a poem. This she read to us.

> I remember standing in Gallarus
> next to the farmhouse where you were born,
> as the cows wandered down the road to pasture.
> I wondered what life was like
> when you were a boy in Dingle.
>
> I remember peering into the cracked window
> of the one room school you attended,
> which you called "The University"
> in your stories of childhood,
> now overgrown with weeds and dust.
>
> I remember, when I returned, your coarse whisper to me
> thin and pale in your hospital bed
> "Those Celtics games,
> those were good times,"
> and mom telling me that was my message.
>
> Then I remembered before we left
> hearing your voice clear and sure
> saying, "I'll be getting my wings soon,
> and flying over Mount Brandon.
> I'll be going home."

Liz told us that as a child she had taken Irish step-dancing lessons for seven years. She slipped off her sandals and apologized for not having the proper tap-like shoes, but pointed out that there wouldn't be much sound anyway on the carpeted floor. The song she had cued up was "Boil the Breakfast Early" from *The Best of the Chieftains* (1992). She pressed *play*: insistent, rapid beating of a goatskin drum began. A tin whistle followed, then a clicking sound, and finally a rousing fiddle. Sometimes the instruments talked back and forth to each other in brief spirited solos; sometimes they blended.

With the music in full tilt, Liz danced a treble reel, her arms extended at her sides, pinned close to her body, her bare feet flying. I rose from my seat in order to see better. And suddenly the whole experience rushed into me—the poem, Liz's voice, the painting, the light reflecting off the flag, the music, and this quiet young woman, erect, upper body still, legs and feet ablur, performing the dance of her ancestors. I was overcome. Susan stood up beside me. Tears sprang into my eyes; Susan's too. We glanced at each other and both knew: This was teacher nirvana.

What, I have wondered, caused this deep emotional response in us? Which genre? Which mode of expression? The poem? The painting? The music? The dance? The brilliant flag of Ireland? This demure young woman using her body to take us back scores of years to the old country? The experience of trying to feel what Liz felt about her grandfather and being Irish? The arts of writing, painting, music, and dance all coming together as one, enhancing each other, informing us, upping the emotional ante, building in a multigenre, multimedia, multidimensional experience?

All of this, I suspect, and Mary, Jesus, and Holy St. Joseph, it was a bright, indelible moment.

Liz's presentation that morning wasn't a multigenre paper in the way that hundreds of my students have written them, but it contained all the elements of one and more. Liz explored her topic in a multitude of ways, and all those ways were linked by her themes of Irish culture and family. She moved us. She moved us through her writing, her voice, her art, her body, her way of perceiving, her very being. We felt her energy, courage, commitment, and passion to express and communicate. The intellectual and the emotional were one.

[handwritten margin note: important elements of writing a paper]

MULTIGENRE BEGINNINGS

The idea of the multigenre paper began to evolve in me in the summer of 1986 when I read Michael Ondaatje's *The Collected Works of Billy the Kid* (1970). Ondaatje wrote about the last years of Billy the Kid's life in a style I'd never read before. Not a collection of poems. Not a seamless narrative. Not an expository biography. The book contained songs, thumbnail character sketches, poems, a comic book excerpt, narrative, stream-of-consciousness passages, newspaper interviews, even photographs and drawings. Ondaatje has called

> I can write a good, safe analytical paper any day. Multigenre is a bit more dangerous. For me, it requires investing myself more. As a result, multigenre is much more rewarding.
>
> Emily Bradshaw, Senior, Brigham Young University

the book a "pre-novel" and also "half theater, half film, half book, half music hall" (Caldwell 1994, 41). I call it "multigenre."

Out of his inquiry into Billy the Kid, Ondaatje created a complex, multilayered, multivoiced blend of genres, each revealing information about his topic, each self-contained, making a point of its own, unconnected to other genres by conventional transitional devices. I cannot emphasize enough this idea of separateness. Each genre is a color slide, complete in itself, possessing its own satisfying composition, but also working in concert with the others to create a single literary experience.

> I was surprised when, through different perspectives, I started writing about feelings and emotions I didn't even know I had.
> Lindsey Dallman, Freshman, Miami University

> I've never done so much thinking about Grammy, and it was wonderful. I got to give her a better characterization through the use of multiple genres. She had a voice in journal form. She received voices in letters. She was poetry and photograph and prose. An expository essay would have limited my expression of the amount of life I believe Grammy possessed.
> Clare Cox, Graduate Student, Miami University

All these genre snapshots combine to re-create part of the *factual* world of Billy the Kid but also the *imaginative* world of dramatic scenes and characters' emotions as we see life unfold without, for the most part, an author's explicit interpretation. Factual and emotional. Objective and subjective. Real and imagined.

[handwritten margin note: Facts & images good multi genre paper]

I was teaching in a high school when I read *The Collected Works of Billy the Kid*, and I began to wonder if my students could write research papers in Michael Ondaatje's multigenre style. They could, of course. Since 1988 I have had students in high school, college, and graduate school write multigenre papers. And they are successful when I provide models of such papers, lead students into prompts that enable them to experiment with various genres and writing strategies, hold conferences with them, and devote class time to the development of their writing within a community of sharing, so everyone can catch the classroom's creative current.

TESTIMONIES

In the last twelve years teachers from grade school through college across the country have taken the idea of multigenre and run with it. They have adapted it, expanded it, made it their own.

I'm always thrilled with the results of the multigenre paper, because students get excited about the assignment, try lots of new writing forms, read and respond to each other's work, revise their drafts, and turn in their best writing of the year. They often do more than required, because they have so much to say . . . and they're experimenting with interesting ways of saying it.

Georgia Swing,
The Marshal School

A primary reason that I use the multigenre format is selfish—the quality of writing that I get to read is often so much truer in its feel. . . . My colleague, Thomi Liebich, states that while reading and research help students to write more convincingly, the power of the multigenre form makes the information real—the "imagination puts some meat on those bones" by creating pictures to go along with the words.

Sirpa Grierson,
Brigham Young University

An e-mail message came to me unexpectedly from a high school teacher in a neighboring school district who had taken a graduate course with me:

Tom, I was sitting here grading the multigenre research papers that my seniors just completed, and I had to tell you how enjoyable they are to grade. I look forward to grading the next one, rather than dreading it. These are not written by top students either, but they are interesting . . . . Traditionalists would never approve of replacing the RESEARCH PAPER, but if the students come out of it enjoying the experience and learning at the same time, it's hard to argue against it.

Laney Bender-Slack,
Mason High School

Another teacher explains how multigenre papers have become stimulants for both her students and herself:

The best things I've discovered are the way the writing becomes so interesting on all levels. Word choice and sentence variety step up at least a notch or two . . . students' inventiveness is triggered. They recognize the interactions between form and meaning.

Conferences that I have with students become so much more fulfilling. They ask really important questions about how to set a concept into a form they are discovering.

I look forward to reading multigenre papers. I hated to read traditional research papers because I had to sit in an uncomfortable chair and literally pinch myself at times to stay focused. Such papers, when well done, revealed the blending of many sources—except for the most important one—the student's voice. I began to resent spending my precious life reading this lackluster writing.

Sue Amendt,
Indiana Area High School

Now it's time you read a multigenre paper.

2 | A PLACE TO START

This chapter features the first of five full multigenre papers, "Cosmetic Clips" by Jennifer Sorensen. Accessible to both high school and college students alike, "Cosmetic Clips" is as an excellent introduction to the multigenre concept.

When I met Jennifer, she was a student in the Theory and Practice of Writing master's degree program at Utah State University. Gaining less and less fulfillment from her job at a department store cosmetic counter, Jennifer enrolled in graduate school so she could make a profound vocational change. The nature of the degree (and the writing culture of USU's English department) encouraged graduate students to write in many genres: fiction, personal essays, technical writing, and poetry as well as academic papers. Jennifer excelled in all of these. She wanted to write, and she also wanted to teach others how to work with words.

While multigenre papers often come out of research in secondary sources, I've learned to wish students Godspeed in pursuing topics that arise from the countryside of the soul. Jennifer's topic cut to the core of her vocational discontent.

COSMETIC CLIPS

For all the Cosmetic Specialists I worked with and knew well.

TODAY IN COSMETICS, NYMENS HAS A SPECIAL GIFT FOR YOU! WITH ANY CLINIQUE PURCHASE OF $12.50 OR MORE YOU WILL RECEIVE ONE BONUS BAG—FREE. OUR COSMETIC SPECIALISTS WOULD LOVE TO SHOW YOU THE LATEST COSMETIC TRENDS. STOP AT LEVEL ONE TODAY AND LET THEM GIVE YOU A COMPLIMENTARY MAKEOVER. REMEMBER AT NYMENS, CUSTOMER SERVICE IS OUR TOP PRIORITY!

The Makeover

My customer looks in the mirror
seeks transformation by an artist's touch.
Layers of blue-red base to hide blemishes,
dark circles, lingering lines.
She tells me about her divorce, failed career,
and a close friend's death—while I blend them away
in the folds of her face, chin, and neck.
I apply gray liner, sketch soft peach shadow and
blush the patch scars; massage regret.
With skilled strokes I make her face even—
like a painted picture—one that has no memory
of an earlier place and time. Beneath blotted
lipstick she smiles while I complete her
portrait with powder.

Beautiful Red Hair

"She had the most beautiful, long, red hair, and the kind of freckles
that go with the red hair—you know the kind I mean."

"The dyed kind or natural red?"

"Natural—anyway, she looked so bad. No makeup and dark
circles under her eyes! I put her in the chair and we started talking.
She looked like she might burst into tears at any moment. She told
me that last week she came home from work—she's a nurse and
works night shifts—and found her husband dead at his computer.
Thirty-two-years-old and he had a heart attack. They have two
young boys and no life insurance."

"Exactly how old are her boys?"

"Two and four—this was the first time she had left her house
since his funeral."

"Did you sell her anything?"

NYMENS TRAINING TIP NUMBER ONE: SUGGESTIVE SELL-
ING IS A MUST! NEVER LET YOUR CUSTOMER LEAVE WITH-
OUT BUYING MORE THAN ONE ITEM. MULTIPLE SALES IS
THE KEY TO SUCCESS!

May I Help You?

"Sandra, how much do you have up?"

"Four hundred, and you?"

"Two, but I've been here longer than you."

"You'll do more soon."

"No way, Sandra."

"See that man in the brown suit standing at the fragrance bar?"
"Yeah."
"Two hundred easy. Watch me."

Wendy's Waltz

She starts by smiling, then she bends over just enough to grab the nearest perfume tester, Oscar. When she does, the man in the brown suit notices how short her black skirt is or perhaps he just likes the way her slim legs look in black panty hose.

"Does the person you are shopping for prefer a floral or a spice fragrance?"

"My wife—girlfriend likes well—what do you like?"

Wendy's high heels click as she walks around the counter and carefully selects Chanel #5, a higher priced fragrance than the one she previously held in her hand.

"I like something in between. This is one that I wear. Would you like me to put some on for you to smell? When you spray fragrance on a fragrance card, often it doesn't smell the same as it does on someone's skin."

Wendy watches the man in the brown suit answer his cellular phone. The whole time he speaks he smiles at her and nods a few times. Wendy leans closer to the man, so he can smell the fragrance where she has sprayed it on her neck. The man's eyes are now on her low-cut, white silk blouse.

"Do you want perfume or parfum?" Wendy whispers to the man.

He finishes his brief phone call and smiles at her. Wendy rubs one hand along her side and then taps her red fingernails against her belt.

"What's the difference?"

"Perfume has more oil in it and therefore lasts longer, especially if you layer it with lotion and powder."

Wendy reaches into the case and pulls out a Chanel lotion and powder and places it on the counter.

"Do you want the full ounce or the half ounce perfume?"

"Why don't you give me the full ounce."

Wendy smiles. She can see Sandra walking toward the fragrance counter.

"Well, your girlfriend is certainly lucky to have a great man like you to spoil her. Would you like me to wrap these for you?"

Sandra is now at the counter next to Wendy.

"Look, Sandra, this man is giving Chanel to his girlfriend."

"I wish it were me—I'm jealous."

"I bet you are," Wendy winks at Sandra and smiles.

"How much did you say everything came to?" the man inquires.

"Only $272.69 with tax, and I've included a free sample of bath gel."

NYMENS TRAINING TIP NUMBER TWO: NEVER LET YOUR CUSTOMERS KNOW THAT YOU WORK ON COMMISSION AND NEVER DISCUSS YOUR SALARY WITH ANOTHER EMPLOYEE. IF YOU ARE CAUGHT DOING EITHER OF THESE THINGS, YOU WILL BE SUSPENDED IMMEDIATELY!

Vanity Keepers

After a hectic work shift, we are restocking merchandise, sacks, and supplies. We are cleaning smeared lipstick, foundation, blush and handprints from the rows of glass cases. We are exhausted; our legs and backs ache from standing all day on tile. Our fingers itch with dryness from continued cleansing between makeovers. Some of our friends envy us because they believe we are beautiful women with perfect skin because we know all the skincare secrets. Men flirt with us; frustrated housewives hate us. We watch some customers spend more money in one hour than some of us earn in one paycheck.

Help Wanted
Nymens' Cosmetic Specialist

Attractive women ages 21–39 with
prior cosmetic experience. Must
have excellent communication skills.
Single, non-mothers preferred.
Must be able to work anytime
Monday–Sunday including holidays.
No wrinkles, age spots, facial
scars or bad teeth. Heavy foundation,
panty hose, high heels and hairspray
required. No sick pay or personal
leave time. Overweight applicants
and applicants with physical
handicaps need not apply. No job
security unless you maintain sales
goals. Aggressive, self-motivated,
persistent women only. Big busted
blondes encouraged to apply.
Actresses and anorexics preferred.
Please contact Sherrie Airs at
231-2343 for an appearance interview.

"Wendy, Ann's school just called and told me to come and pick her up. She's got a fever—probably the flu. What am I going to do? Jake's out of town and I have no one to leave her with."

"Sue will never let you go. We're shorthanded in the department today. Have you taken your lunch yet?"

"No, why?"

"Take a long lunch—I'll try to cover for you. Then call Sue right before she leaves to go home and tell her you have car trouble and you'll be in as soon as you can."

"Do you think it'll work?"

"Do you have any other options? Remember Amie? She got fired at the first of the week because she left when her daughter was sick."

"Thanks, Wendy. I owe you one."

NYMENS TRAINING TIP NUMBER THREE: DON'T ACCEPT CUSTOMER RETURNS WITHOUT EXCHANGING THE MERCHANDISE FOR SOMETHING ELSE. REMEMBER, RETURNS ARE SUBTRACTED FROM YOUR MONTHLY COMMISSION.

Stacey

Everyone knows that Stacey is the perfect wife, mother, church leader, and Nymen's top-selling cosmetics specialist. Petite and attractive, Stacey is never late for work and makes more commission than any other coworker on her cosmetic line. She works past her shift even when the cosmetic manager doesn't ask her to, and she never takes breaks. Stacey is always pleasant and knows all her customers by name. No one knows that Stacey steals: when they are not around, she takes her coworkers' holds (merchandise they have either selected for or helped a customer with and are waiting for the customer to return and purchase) and rings them up on her own number so she can get their commission, she often enters her cosmetic line codes into the register instead of the actual ones so her sales appear to be bigger, she puts extra testers from the stockroom in her pockets and takes them home, and she snatches money from unattended employee wallets. No one has caught on to the creative accounting methods she uses when she balances her line book. In the six years that Stacey has worked for Nymens, she has stolen over $25,000.

Doing Books

All day long we're doing books doing books
All day adding columns, sales and profits
Red for sold, blue transfers, green orders—
Not enough red. All of us doing books doing
Books. Can't leave until our columns match
The sales reports—they must match the columns
Sold—but we struggle to get our columns to match.
There can be no errors—we fight tension, anxiety,
Stress and headaches until the final figure
When we finish doing books doing books all day
Long we're doing books.

Reflection

My husband told me this morning that I have become hard, almost
plastic—like a Barbie doll. Instantly, I was angry, then the tears
came. He was the one who wanted me to make more money. Why
doesn't he understand how hard it is—how hard I work? What
would he be like if he were under constant pressure to sell or be
fired. He says I'm not as much fun to be around as I used to be. I
look in the mirror and I see a tired woman with too much
makeup—suddenly I don't know who I am anymore.

Returner's Strategy

If I empty the Clinique foundation I bought yesterday at Nymens
into another bottle, and fill this one with water, then I can return
it to Nymens tomorrow and get enough money to buy the new shirt
I wanted for the party on Saturday. I'll just tell the saleswomen I'm
allergic to it and I'll still get to keep the free gift.

NYMENS TRAINING TIP NUMBER FOUR: REMEMBER, THE
CUSTOMER IS ALWAYS RIGHT. DON'T DO ANYTHING TO
JEOPARDIZE NYMENS' EXCELLENT CUSTOMER RAPPORT.

Circles

When I sell, sell, sell
I make more, more, more
And I'm happy, happy, happy
Until next year when I have to sell
More, more, more to beat the sales
I did this year in order to keep
My job, job, job.

My Mommy Sells Lipstick

"Jackie, I'm depressed. Yesterday Dylan came home from school and asked me what I do. He explained that Billy's mom is a nurse and Alan's mom works for Novell. I started to say that I used to be a teacher—that teaching was something I loved to do and how rewarding it was to teach fifth grade but the pay wasn't very good and Nymens pays more—but then I just looked at him and answered, "Your mommy sells lipstick."

Dear Nymens Valued Customer,

I must confess that I was immensely disappointed that you did not purchase more during our Holiday Makeover Madness Weekend. After all, do you really think I pamper you because I like you? I have to make a living too!

You only bought one blush and then you had the nerve to return it on Monday. So I wasted a half an hour on you when I could have made more commission assisting someone else. Big mistake! And I'm sick of hearing about the Italian lover you met during an EST meeting. Who cares?

Anyway, about all the free samples I've been giving you—well I need them back. I need them for my real customers—you know the ones who buy two hundred dollars in my line each time they come in and don't return anything.

Please do me a favor and change cosmetic lines.

Your Cosmetic Specialist,

Louise

At the Cemetery

December 7. It's cold and windy. We only have an hour for lunch. When Sandra and I get out of the car we can hear LeAnna wailing, "Not my baby. My beautiful baby." LeAnna is pacing around the grave site. She is dressed completely in black, and she is wearing sunglasses, no makeup; her face is stark white. The snow crunches under our feet as we move to keep warm and place red roses on the tiny casket. "Not my baby," LeAnna's voice echoes over and over in the wind. Sudden Infant Death Syndrome.

Back at Nymens

During the return drive no one speaks. I'm remembering how aggressive LeAnna is on the sales floor. How easily she takes customers from me if I turn my back for even a minute; how perfect her makeup always is.

When we return to the cosmetic department, Sandra and I notice two fat women tugging on the same fragile fragrance wreath—each one arguing that she had it first. There's no time to waste. We have to sell at least two hundred dollars to the demanding Nymens holiday shoppers before the end of our shift.

I Want to Retire

In the mirrors around the cosmetics counter I see wrinkles under my eyes that I've never noticed before, a small run in my new panty hose, my hips bigger today, my uniform falling apart, my lipstick smeared, my shoes wearing out, and my hair turning gray.

I'm not perfect.

Perhaps I'm too old for this job.

THANK YOU FOR SHOPPING AT NYMENS WHERE OUR NUMBER ONE GOAL IS TO PLEASE YOU. DON'T FORGET TO STOP AT OUR COSMETICS DEPARTMENT ON LEVEL ONE. TODAY IS THE LAST DAY OF OUR CLINIQUE BONUS GIFT. JUST PURCHASE $12.50 OR MORE AND YOU WILL RECEIVE THE BONUS BAG—FREE!

3 | TEACHER EXPERTISE
Timing

If I was talking to the next group of students doing a multigenre paper, I would tell them to give it time. Don't try to rush yourself through the process. Allow development; you'll be happier with the final product.

Eric Weiss, Sophomore,
Miami University

We teachers are often concerned with logistics and timing: when will we read this, write that, meet in groups, spend time in the library, discuss a particular issue, take that evening graduate class. If students often ask teachers how long a piece of writing should be, teachers often ask themselves how long a project or unit should take.

Teachers who lead their students to write multigenre papers approach this issue in many ways. Here are some of their solutions to the issue of time and curriculum:

High school teacher Mary Rollinger's multigenre unit lasts six to eight weeks, a time when she teaches students "genre by genre what each is and how to locate samples and create their own." Mary sets a week-by-week deadline for each genre.

Sirpa Grierson of Brigham Young University has a similar pedagogical philosophy for keeping students in her young adult literature class on track as they write their multigenre papers about an author or character from YA

Sources for the Alternate Style (Grammar B)

These books show how writers, teachers, and students have broken rules of standard English and written powerfully. The freedom and confidence that students develop when trying some of these alternate style maneuvers feeds perfectly into multigenre explorations, which are themselves an altering of style.

BISHOP, WENDY, ed. 1997. *Elements of Alternate Style: Essays on Writing and Revision.* Portsmouth, NH: Heinemann-Boynton/Cook.

ROMANO, TOM. 1995. *Writing with Passion.* (Chapters 5 & 6) Portsmouth, NH: Heinemann-Boynton/Cook.

WEATHERS, WINSTON. 1980. *An Alternate Style: Options in Composition.* Rochelle Park, NJ: Hayden Book Company. OP.

lit. Two or three weeks into the course she introduces students to writers like Michael Ondaatje and John Dos Passos and the work of other writers who have successfully used alternate style strategies like double voice, repetition, and labyrinthine sentences. Students then have eight to ten weeks to develop their papers. Each Monday Sirpa introduces students to a strategy or genre. On Wednesday students bring drafts to class for peer response. Although students don't have to use every piece they've tried out, the weekly writing generates more writing and ideas. Sirpa also increases the legitimacy of this weekly writing by grading each piece.

Sirpa knows, too, the value of an outside voice for inspiring her students. A guest speaker about multigenre is an important part of the classroom work.

> As we approach the end of the first month of class, I try to invite my friend and colleague Thomi Liebich to class to talk about his experiences in writing a multigenre paper using Holden in J. D. Salinger's *Catcher in the Rye.* Having Thomi speak is one of the most effective things that I have done as he is able to relate the process that he went through to create his writings about Holden and, while reading, also share the visual impact of his writing with us. The opportunity to listen to and question a writer who understands multigenre is very powerful. Thomi is able to articulate things in a manner that inspires students to write on a deeper level.

The time students spend on the multigenre project varies depending on the other demands of the curriculum and the teacher's goals. Although Sirpa spends a large chunk of time getting college students to develop their papers, Melinda Putz of Ithaca High School in Michigan gives her eleventh-grade mixed-ability students four weeks to write multigenre research papers. She notes that

> students do not have the entire period each day for individual work. We either do Daily Oral Language together or have a mini-lesson on an alternate style technique with a few minutes to try one out. Following this, we go to the media center to research with books or with computers.

Sue Amendt of Indiana Area High School in Indiana, Pennsylvania, likes to allow at least five weeks for multigenre work.

> We usually are doing more than one thing at a time, so we do that "other thing" (like read common pieces together, or work on our portfolios, or create a class booklet) two or three times a week depending on which project is most needy. Often the students decide this as they are the needy ones. Class is a workshop, so some go to the library or dig through the cart of resource books that I have on

loan from the school library. Some do response work or, if others are working on a related topic, swap info and perspectives. Others who are in trouble hang around my desk eavesdropping on conferences that I am having with others about their successes, failures, and stuck points with the paper.

The necessity of coordinating time lines amid other curricular responsibilities has proved to be the biggest headache for Becky Hoag of Tom C. Clark High School in San Antonio. "The first student evaluations said, 'Give us a syllabus,'" she writes, "so now I do." This syllabus provides an overview of the project and notes guidelines, requirements, assignments, and their due dates.

4 | THE DAMP OF THE NIGHT

Theory about narrative thinking provides scholarly underpinning for multigenre writing. I came across such theory in the work of Jerome Bruner (1986) a year and a half after my high school students wrote multigenre papers. In this chapter I want to share that theory with you and my personal connection to it as a teacher and writer. I'll begin by telling an action research story. I wanted to learn how my English methods students would respond to different genres of writing about the same subject.

Here is the first piece I gave to them, an entry from *Webster's American Biographies* (1975):

Basie, William (1904–[1984]), "Count," musician. Born in Red Bank, New Jersey, on August 21, 1904, William Basie was musically inclined from childhood. In his teens he studied piano, for a time with Fats Waller, who also taught him to play the organ and got him into vaudeville as an accompanist. For a few years he played on the East Coast and then worked his way west until he was stranded in Kansas City, Missouri. There he joined Walter Page's "Blue Devils" and then Benny Moten's band, at the time the leading jazz group in the Midwest. Soon after Moten's death in 1935, Basie formed his own band with Page, Freddy Green, Jo Jones, Lester Young, and others. The band played at the Reno Club in Kansas City and, although it was short on formal arrangements, soon attracted a considerable following with its driving rhythm and brilliant solo work. A chance hearing of one of their local radio broadcasts by an influential jazz enthusiast led to their traveling to New York City in 1936 and to a recording contract the following year. Engagements at a series of fashionable clubs, theaters, and hotels quickly established the band as one of the most popular in the country and recordings spread their fame throughout the world. A succession of great soloists . . . and vocalists . . . helped to keep the appeal of Count Basie's music growing; always it was characterized by the trademark "jumping" beat and the contrapuntal accents of Basie's own piano. The band broke up in 1950 and for a year or so Basie toured with a small combo. . . . In 1951 he organized a new big band and immediately surpassed his earlier success in a number of tours across the county and in Europe. . .

After we read the bio, I asked students to write what they had learned about Count Basie. Diana's writing represents typical information the students gathered:

Count Basie was musically inclined from childhood. He wandered around playing in various cities. He joined the "Blue Devils" before forming his own band with some other guys. When the band broke up, Basie toured with a small group. In 1951, he formed a new big band. This band was more successful than any of the others. He became known as one of the great big band leaders.

Diana Rainey, Junior,
Miami University

Count Basie died when these students were five or six, so I shouldn't have been surprised when several of them admitted they had never heard of Basie. Shelly knew he had been a jazz musician but was surprised to learn he was American; she figured he was foreign (like Count Dracula). Leah speculated that he got his title because he was "talented, esp on the piano." Evie noted that the entry didn't mention Basie's race, which she thought was a grievous omission, since part of why he was so important, she believed, was his influence in bringing the Big Band sound to African Americans. Alan—our dual English and music major—wrote that Basie was not as accepted as the entry suggests. Many students noted that Basie had been a child prodigy, and half of them mentioned the "trademark 'jumping' beat" of his band, whatever that meant.

Students, I saw, had learned things about Count Basie from their brief transaction with the expository text. One student, however, wrote about what wasn't in the bio:

This is just a factual account of a musical legend. It's hard to put into words the things a guy like Count Basie could do with a musical instrument. When I think of Count Basie, I think Zoot Suits and hepcats and wild dancing and unbelievable live music atmosphere.

Tom Myers, Junior,
Miami University

Tom knew there was more to understanding Count Basie than knowing the year he was born, the city where he got his start, and the names of famous musicians he worked with. Tom's response anticipated my next pedagogical move. I gave students a far different genre about Basie—a poem. I asked them to listen as I read and then to jot down emotions and feelings that came through to them.

Basic Basie

Hunched . humped backed . gigantic
the pianist presides above the
rumpus . his fingers clutch the

chords . dissonance and dischord vie
and vamp across the key
board

his big feet beat the beat until the whole joint
rocks . it is not romantic
but a subtile fingering exudes a sweet exotic

fragrance now and then . you'll
recognize the flagrance if you listen
well . this flower blooms and blossoms . till

brash boogie woogie hordes come bourgeoning up from hell
blind
and gigantic

Kamau Brathwaite

"This is what I'm talking about," wrote Tom. "We shape sound of music with these words. Count Basie was hypnotic. I keep thinking about *The Autobiography of Malcolm X* [by Alex Haley]. The author describes the Harlem night club scene and my heart is just pounding."

Students went beyond the facts of Basie's career to gain a visceral sense of him when he was doing what made his life sweet upon this earth:

"Frantic, dancing—hedonistic, but beautiful," wrote Clare. "Basie is the master—presiding 'above the rumpus.' Music is the driving factor and source of emotion. Music and rhythm so powerful it gets into your soul."

Tonia wrote, "I get that he was a large man who played his music passionately with a mood of lost loves, blues, and good times."

"He's a big guy," wrote Jenn, "plays with passion, seemed to draw his music up from the depth of hell. His music overtakes your senses like a beautiful flower . . . . Makes me want to dance."

In Diana—whose fact-gathering paragraph I quoted earlier—the poem produced kinesthetic imagery in body and mind: "I can feel the pounding of the keyboard in my chest. I picture Basie laboring away at the piano, a performance in some smoky bar while people rock back & forth in their seats, the music pumping through his veins onto the keyboard, into the ears of the listeners."

Ryan fingered what the poem did that the biographical sketch did not: "You could hear the 'jumping' beat."

Brathwaite's poem bloods Count Basie. It moves him beyond names, dates, and chronology. The poem renders the Basie persona, draws readers into imagining what it might have been like to attend a Basie performance.

After the brief writing, students engaged in exploratory small-group conversation and then spirited large-group discussion. The writing and listening and wide-range talking propelled Clare to a metaphorical leap: "The 'boogie woogie hordes,'" she said, "are people who just can't keep themselves from dancing." Several students talked about the demonic aspect of Basie's music, how alluring and exotic it was, how enticing. Kasie said that the music was "all-encompassing—small as flowers, big as hell," that Basie himself was "ogre-like, hunched, humped-backed, gigantic."

After the discussion, we wrote briefly again about what we now knew of Count Basie.

Amy hearkened to Alan's point that Basie's music was not readily accepted: "People may not have welcomed it at first because it had a new message and tone," she wrote, "but it enticed them to join in dancing and moving, the music's sound so powerful that people who tried not to listen gave in. A powerful man who played powerful music."

And Leah wrote that Basie's music was "strong enough and beautiful enough (flower blooms) to encourage even the demons of hell to appreciate it. The music is so catching it's almost evil. People can't help but indulge in the pleasure."

Now, I thought, now, students knew something of the Count's passion and distinctive presence at the piano. Now they knew something of Count Basie.

Don't get me wrong. I'm not ready to toss out expository writing, even though my students responded with enthusiasm and emotion to "Basic Basie," even though Brathwaite's imagery, alliteration, rhythm, and inventive language unleashed more interesting writing and thinking in them than the factual exposition. I don't dismiss the biographical entry, don't compare it to "Basic Basie" and find it lacking. The thumbnail bio is simply different. We're talking apples and kiwi here, the Galápagos Islands and Iowa farm land, Georgia O'Keefe and Pablo Picasso. The bio was written for different reasons than the poem, was driven by different purposes, is doing different rhetorical work.

If I were investigating Count Basie, the piece from *Webster's American Biographies* would be a good place to start my research. It is a densely packed, backyard garden of information. It informs me about important people in Basie's life, all of whom I could track down to see further how their lives influenced his. I learn about a singular "jumping" quality to Basie's music that surely would send me to the record store. I see the chronology of Basie's musical life unfold, understand its progression from band member to Big Band icon, get a sense of Basie's professional resiliency. And the entry does this in concise prose with active verbs (Basie *studied, played, worked, joined, formed*). The one use of passive voice, in fact, is eminently appropriate. When Basie, just twenty-one years old, "was stranded" in Kansas City, that had to be the proverbial darkness before dawn breaks and his career takes off. (Kansas City, it turns out, was an excellent place for a young jazz musician to be stranded in the 1930s.)

The biographical entry is journeyman informational writing that has an irreplaceable function in our world. We couldn't get along without it. But, oh! Do I like Brathwaite's poem. And I'm betting that the image of Basie in command at the piano with scores of faceless, possessed figures lindy-hopping to his music will last longer in me than the name of the first band Basie joined in Kansas City.

The poem and the bio are doing different work, and the ways that Brathwaite and the anonymous bio writer saw and communicated are different as well. The bio is concerned with reportage, facts, analysis, chronology, and logic. Jerome Bruner called such "thinking" *paradigmatic* (1986). We find it in textbooks, editorials, news stories, academic papers, articles, even in the talk of children trying to persuade their parents that they should be able to go swimming on the first day the pool is open, even though it is sixty-two degrees and windy. Paradigmatic thinking is all around us, and it's indispensable.

But it isn't the only way to think, although it might appear so given the emphasis that secondary schools and higher education give it. Another way to know that Bruner writes about is *narrative*: stories, poetry, drama, even painting and movement. Instead of explaining or analyzing as paradigmatic knowing does, narrative knowing renders experience or phenomenon. Narrative knowing shows. We read a novel and leave the world. We read a poem and feel a sharp, emotional surge. We see a painting and meld into it. We dream of falling and jolt ourselves awake.

After junior high school—sometimes before—school is devoted to teaching students to think paradigmatically. The predominant mode of writing is exposition. There is little sanction in expository school for narrative knowing, unless it is written by someone published. Many teachers do not consider writing poetry or fiction cognitively rigorous. So the irony persists that while teachers might read plenty of imaginative literature—even revere it as some of the best word work people have produced—they funnel students' writing in its opposite direction.

I am an agent against such thinking.

Like many students today, as a teenager I was pretty much a Johnny-One-Genre. I wrote exposition about the concerns of others: summaries of authors' lives, argumentative essay answers in which I refurbished a teacher's lecture notes, and reports about books, historical events, and scientific experiments. In four years of high school English and as an English major in college, although I *read* plenty of fiction, poetry, and exploratory essays, I did not write those genres. My way of seeing and saying through the written word—what school required of me—was expository, was paradigmatic, was, I have come to recognize, academic in the worst sense (i.e., excessively abstract).

I am an agent against such thinking.

During my first semester of college in 1967 at Miami University in Ohio, I struck a friendship with a dormitory mate from Cincinnati. We had the same teacher for freshman writing, although Tom's SAT scores had placed him in an accelerated section. He showed me a paper he'd written in which he told a story about driving over to pick up his friends. The characters spoke and acted; the story seemed aimless and leisurely. Inscribed at the top of the paper was an "A." I was confused. Tom had explained nothing. This was college, I thought, not junior high school. Where, I wondered, was the thesis? The pro and con arguments? The point-by-point submission of the opposition? The summary in the final paragraph containing a restatement of the thesis? Missing were they all. Tom's so-called advanced section of freshman English was anything but. I was indignant, felt slighted and a little righteous. From what my new East Coast college acquaintances were telling me, advanced freshman English at Miami was a little like Harvard: the difficult part was getting admitted.

Tom's personal narrative that read like fiction was my first look at another student's writing that wasn't an expository essay. And I retain an image from that writing these many years later almost as vivid as Count Basie presiding above the rumpus. Tom had engaged in an alternate way of seeing and saying from the paradigmatic. He'd demonstrated a different way of being in the world with words, another way of understanding experience, a way I was familiar with, after all, through my reading of fiction and poetry. The orthodoxies of my own school experience, however, had militated against students expressing themselves in those genres. At eighteen I hadn't recognized "narrative knowing" as something I might incorporate into my own academic life.

I am an agent against such thinking.

I can thank the late Milton White for that. I finally found him my junior year at Miami and enrolled in his beginning fiction writing course, a big risk for expository Tom. But I was fired with moral issues of the heart that novelists dramatized, and eight years earlier I realized I found pleasure putting words on paper. Furthermore, I had enough ego to believe that others wanted to hear the stories I could tell. While Milton sanctioned our stories and kept us riding our personal passions, he beseeched us to "say it simply," to go easy with adverbs, to dramatize scenes, and to avoid telling readers what to think. Instead, he urged, show them with such indelible detail that they go beyond understanding what they have read to experiencing it.

Ever since I learned and grew under Milton's tutelage, I have been showing not telling. I have been—as Peter Elbow (1990) calls it—*rendering* experience, both real and imagined. Narrative thinking is my primary way of knowing the world. Analysis often comes slow to me. I am not the quickest at adding things up. Narrative, however, is my calculator. I often have to tell a story in detail—render it fully—in order to know what it means, in order to come to paradigmatic thinking about it. Although my students do their share of analytical writing, they do a fair amount of narrative knowing through imaginative genres, too. And in all their writing, regardless of the genre, I urge students to use the strategies, techniques, and language ways of imaginative writing.

As I have shaped, extended, and communicated my world through non-expository genres, I have beckoned students to do the same. And I've felt occasional twinges of guilt for this. Shouldn't I be devoting more time to teaching exposition so students get ready to write essay tests, reports, and term papers? The guilt, in fact, is still with me as I encounter so many teachers—at least in Ohio—who shamelessly tout the five-paragraph essay, a form they feel students must master in order to pass the state writing proficiency tests. It doesn't matter that this form does not exist outside the narrow culture of test taking and the classrooms that endorse it. No matter that Janet Emig (1972) debunked the "five-star essay," as she called it, nearly thirty years ago.

Despite my guilt, however, I have persisted in getting students to engage in narrative thinking, to experience how it can enhance their expository writing, to expand their essays beyond five paragraphs with engaging leads, illuminating anecdotes, sharp dialog, and implicitly emphatic conclusions.

THE DAMP OF THE NIGHT

In most of my writing the cognitive and the emotional are entwined. This happens because in whatever I write, I seek a place for narrative thinking. More than I am interested in reflecting on or abstracting from experience, I am interested in rendering it so that readers live the page. When done well, Tom Newkirk (1997) contends, such rendering "penetrates" experience (95), taking readers inside a present moment, *present* because narrative thinking lets us experience the writing, a little like watching a compelling movie or Count Basie presiding above the rumpus or Liz Irish step dancing.

We find experience penetrated in poetry, fiction, and plays. Louise Rosenblatt (1978) says that literature offers readers a chance to engage in a "lived through experience," an experience that has been penetrated. In such writing it is often solely up to readers to reflect upon meaning and make abstractions. Authors of narrative thinking ask readers to live the page. And we leave the world. Essays, too, of course, may contain narrative thinking, though often they do not. Exceptions that come to mind are essays by Andre Dubus (1994) and Barbara Kingsolver (1995), both of whom are primarily fiction writers, I should note.

Multigenre papers, however, as I conceive them, *demand* that writers think narratively. Writers must meld the cognitive with the emotional. Long ago Walt Whitman wrote

Logic and sermons never convince,
the damp of the night drives deeper into my soul.

Whitman's words have carried me for years. But they don't carry everyone: "I don't believe that," said a friend of mine. John knows that logic and sermons *can* convince and cited as an example Atticus Finch's summation at Tom Robinson's trial in *To Kill a Mockingbird*. The logic and reason are persuasive and compelling, John maintains. I think so too. But there is this to consider: Prior to Atticus Finch uttering a word of his eloquent summation, Harper Lee had rendered and penetrated the mores and character of Maycomb County, Alabama. Readers were primed with narrative knowing before they ever got to the courtroom. So although I admit that *never convince* is overstated, I stand by the spirit of Whitman's meaning.

In reflecting upon his multigenre paper, one college student wrote, "I was forced to consider the nature of and the emotions behind the material I was reporting." In addition to fact, logical thinking, and analysis—the dry light of the day—the multigenre paper made him address "the damp of the night."

My first year teaching at Miami University, I had my methods students write multigenre papers about some aspect of teaching English. One student researched "English as a second language." She wanted to find solutions to problems she might face in the classroom. In addition to learning teaching strategies and theories, she also discovered the *emotional* life of ESL students, largely through Danling Fu's enraging and triumphant ethnography, *My Trouble Is My English* (1995). The student took a metaphor that Fu suggests and wrote a poem in the voice of an ESL student. As Danling wrote to me after reading the poem, "Your student makes the metaphor beautiful and subtle":

Write now
The running sap
Running trapped
In my far dark heart
Is pulsing with spring
But in my mouth
Full of English words
It is still winter

Archer Siggers Neal, Junior,
Miami University

As I said earlier, don't get me wrong. I have nothing against expository writing. Quite the contrary, in fact. I love expository writing when the prose is accessible and vigorous, the thinking irresistible, the whole piece artfully explicit. But I sure love writing that demands an imaginative leap of the reader, writing that is, I like to say, "implicitly emphatic." In her lyrical poem, for example, Archer asks readers to transact with the metaphor of spring and winter and to then understand the yawning chasm that ESL students often face between what they feel and what they are able to express in the foreign language.

Genres of narrative thinking require writers to be concrete and precise. They can't just *tell* in abstract language. They can't just be paradigmatic. They must show. They must make their topics palpable. They must penetrate. And that is what multigenre papers enable their authors to do.

5 | STARTING OUT, MULTIGENRE MODELS, WORKSHOP ROUTINE

Here is how you might introduce students to multigenre writing. Adapt as you see fit.

Day One

Share the encyclopedia entry and poem about Count Basie (Chapter 4). Have students explore their thinking through writing after reading aloud each piece. Then discuss as a large class what each genre is doing; what each writer achieves with language and information; image and rhythm, denotation and connotation.

Day Two

Share an entire multigenre paper in class. I like to use oral interpretation. Such dramatic reading presents the full power of multigenre. Students volunteer (and I do some cajoling) to read various parts or genres. If possible, let students rehearse their parts. The better they inflect their voices, read with appropriate rhythm, and make their personas emotionally convincing, the more effective the multigenre paper will be. I've had Amy Wilson's "Finding Strengths in Our Differences" (Chapter 13) "performed" in scores of classes and workshops.

Amy's work explores a serious contemporary issue, so be sure to spend plenty of time discussing the paper's meanings and implications. But also take time to discuss its form, taking note of the various genres and personas that Amy creates.

Once you get copies of multigenre papers from previous classes, turn students loose on them for further reading. The more experience students have reading multigenre papers—the deeper they become immersed in this form—the greater their subconscious awareness of multigenre possibilities becomes.

Day Three

Topic choice workshop. Share the topics that others have written about. Share topics that you might write a multigenre paper about. Set students to mapping/clustering/brainstorming on paper topics of personal interest. Share these ideas in small groups. Instruct students to generate a lot of talk about writing possibilities. The classroom ought to be abuzz with animated chatter. The more talk writers do about possible topics at this stage, the more cognizant and committed they will become to an area of interest.

Day Four

Students submit their chosen topic in writing with a brief rationale explaining why this subject is suitable for digging into with creative, imaginative, and intellectual energy.

Let students talk about their topics in small groups (with new groupings, perhaps). Peers can help the writer generate ideas for writing and suggest possible sources for research, if that is required of a topic.

After the groups meet, you might ask students to write an addendum to their rationale before collecting them. Respond to these papers by asking questions and suggesting possible genres, research sources, and writing strategies. Above all, validate students' topic choices.

Day Five

Begin multigenre writing workshop in earnest.

MODELS

You might precede students' multigenre writing with a class reading and discussion of a book written in a multitude of genres. I can recommend four titles:

Avi. 1991. *Nothing but the Truth*. New York: Avon. Appropriate for junior high school and above. We see what happens when a school incident is blown out of proportion and different points of view act upon half-truths and misinformation. Written in memos, letters, diary entries, conversations, speeches, newspaper items.

Draper, Sharon. 1994. *Tears of a Tiger*. New York: Atheneum. Appropriate for junior high and above. Novel about urban African American teenagers coping with the ramifications of drunken driving. Accessible and readable. Draper, 1997 National Teacher of the Year, is a veteran teacher in Cincinnati Public Schools. The story unfolds through letters, dialog, newspaper accounts, poems, student homework assignments, even a five-paragraph essay.

Ondaatje, Michael. 1984. *The Collected Works of Billy the Kid.* New York: Penguin. 1970. Original edition, Toronto: House of Anansi Press. Violence and brief explicit sexual passages make this book appropriate for mature high school students and adults. I used this book twice with high school juniors and seniors without parent complaint. (See Chapter 8 in *Writing with Passion.*) A complex and compelling book that is all the more rewarding if contrasted with factual accounts of the life of Billy the Kid. Readers see how Ondaatje takes historical material and writes about it imaginatively.

Ondaatje, Michael. 1976. *Coming Through Slaughter.* Toronto, Canada: General Publishing Co. Limited. Not exactly multigenre but rather a sophisticated, fragmented, impressionistic narrative. The story of jazz coronetist Buddy Bolden around the turn of the century in New Orleans, rendering both his genius and his mental instability. The book features a rewarding example of a recurring phrase.

By all means, share with your students the full papers I have included in this book by Jennifer, Melinda, Jacqui, Jeff, and Amy. And when your students begin to produce multigenre papers, save copies so that future students can read them to broaden their understanding.

WHAT MY MULTIGENRE WEEK LOOKED LIKE IN HIGH SCHOOL

- Monday: Share learning journal/genre experiments in small peer groups. This jump-starts students and gets them talking and thinking about their topics again after the weekend. Workshop follows: writing, reading, viewing, research. Teacher confers with individual students.
- Tuesday: Workshop. Mini-lesson, usually the introduction of a writing strategy or genre that students might use. Most of the time I take five, ten, or fifteen minutes for students to actually try the strategy and share a few of the drafts they generate. A mini-lesson might consist of reading some dialog exchanges, then trying our own hands at dialog. (See Chapter 11.) The bulk of my time after this writing activity is consumed with conferring with writers individually or in small groups. Students engage in writing, reading, viewing, research, occasional conferences with each other.
- Wednesday: Workshop
- Thursday: Workshop.
- Friday: Workshop. Spend twenty or thirty minutes this last day of the week having students read the genre experiments they have under way and passages from their learning journals.

I often hesitate to instruct teachers in how to do the work of their teaching. I know that we have different ways of urging our students to productive work, just as writers have different ways of writing. John Irving wants to know the ending of a book before he starts to write the first chapter. E. L. Doctorow begins writing in earnest only when he knows he has the voice of a character. Once he has that he writes to see how the novel will turn out.

You'll adapt the rhythms of your classroom to meet both your needs and your students'. The attitude you take in launching the multigenre paper for the first time will go a long way in determining the success of the students' work. Nanci Bush presented herself to students as an explorer and co-learner when she introduced them to multigenre writing. She has been devoted to the project ever since:

> My students reacted very positively to the multigenre papers. I think this had a lot to do with their general attitude and my honesty with the process of teaching. I was up-front with the students in my first attempt at teaching multigenre papers; I was quick to say, "I don't know. Try it and see what happens." That allowed a good deal of freedom. The final results branched off in interesting ways.
>
> Nanci Bush,
> Solon High School

6 | TEACHER EXPERTISE
Requirements and Strictures

Teachers are great translators of theory into practice. Writing instruction does not look exactly the same in one classroom as it does in another. And teachers feel varying strictures and freedoms in their own departments and school districts. I asked teachers if they'd had to impose any requirements on their multigenre assignments because of curricular demands or their own educational philosophy.

Brittany Ballard (1998) teaches at Mount Notre Dame High School in Cincinnati. She requires her freshmen to write papers composed of at least six pieces and no more than eight. Two of the pieces must be what she calls major works—at least two typed pages—such as a narrative or play. "That means," Brittany tells students, "that you have to make decisions about what information to include and what to leave out." She asks students to pay attention to "how much," a dilemma that every writer faces:

> You should also have a sense of unity in the whole project. We want to move easily from one piece to the next. In Laura's project about Tina Turner, for example, she used quotes sometimes to connect one piece to the next. You want to do the same thing. You can use pictures, graphs, diagrams, song lyrics, quotations, or interesting facts between the pieces.

Nanci Bush of Solon High School in Ohio makes slightly different requirements:

> A few basic parameters that I set just to answer students' questions included the magic number five: five sources, five genres, five pages. (It was quite a negotiable number, but the students seemed more comfortable having some idea what I was looking for.) Also, I stressed that students connect the genres in some way either with a repetend or by structure.

Sandy Nesvig teaches eighth graders at Annunciation School in Minneapolis. She requires that students have at least eight entries using five different genres. Some students wouldn't experiment as much as I'd like them to without the requirement of different genres. I have also told them that at least six of the entries must be written. Many of them do picture collages as well as drawings, which are often very well done, but I also wanted information. Over the years I have focused more on the papers being informative. I was getting many wonderful letters, diary entries, poetry, etc., but they didn't necessarily show research.

Some teachers feel strong responsibility to departmental requirements to teach research skills. Sue Amendt requires "an annotated working bibliography":

I want to see how students used their sources, and ease my conscience; plus, I want to make them accountable for actually knowing what the one or two bogus sources that they barely used were about. Our department requires MLA format.

One of Sue's students, Aaron Craven, wrote a multigenre paper from the point of view of a German newspaper man who spent World War I on Germany's home front. Here is a sample from his annotated bibliography:

Remarque, Erich Maria. *All Quiet on the Western Front.* United States of America: Ballantine Books, 1982.

In this book I gained a lot of information of what it would have been like to fight on the Western Front. There were a lot of accounts of what the fighting was like, and how the men handled life in the German military. This probably was one of the most important books that I read for this project.

Sometimes requirements for multigenre papers arise from a teacher's own educational philosophy, involving more than logistical matters of uniformity, documentation, and propriety. Sirpa Grierson, for example, writes that

the one thing I require is that students use multiple media. I teach Howard Gardner's multiple intelligence theories in all my classes . . . I want students to incorporate more than just writing into their work—pictures, tactile objects, whatever will help other students to learn about their subject.

Your teaching of the multigenre paper will take on the contours of your district, department, and classroom culture. Add to that the wonderful, personal idiosyncrasies of your students. If your students have room to soar, many will.

7 | OPENERS

Twelve years ago as I read the first multigenre research papers from high school students, I remember my delight changing to discomfort. Then I experienced that falling-away sensation in the bowels. Nothing gradual about this. I've felt it asudden when I've discovered a betrayal, been jilted, forgotten something critical, or learned of the unexpected death of someone I loved. I've felt it, too, when a student has written poorly or learned inadequately and it was my fault.

What caused that feeling twelve years ago was this: After reading a few multigenre papers that pleased and surprised me with invention and voice, I came upon one that confused and stranded me. Reading that paper was like the fright and disorientation I felt as a child my first time in a carnival fun house. I knew that if I wanted the experience to end, I had to keep moving forward. Only by going where I didn't want to go would I emerge into sunlight and be done with the pitch, labyrinthine tunnel and sudden bursts of sound.

I didn't have fun in the fun house, and I didn't have fun reading that paper either, especially since I felt implicated in its failure. Grimly, I finished it, responded to it, and graded it, then went on to several more rewarding papers before I encountered another confusing one. These writers might have known their subject matter, but they presumed too much knowledge on my part, not uncommon in student papers of any kind. The two papers confused me from the first page. I could never find meaningful stability, and I couldn't add up the various genres.

I've since learned to help students think about creating an opening piece that's reader-friendly, informative, and engaging. Multigenre papers defy most readers' expectations. Multigenre writers, therefore, must be doubly careful to orient readers quickly and supply information that will help them build meaning the further they read.

I do this in two ways: I ask students to write a preface, foreword, or introduction that contextualizes the topic of their paper. Writers might tell about the genesis of the paper or of the importance of its subject matter. They

---

Writing a Preface, Foreword, or Introduction

As students near the end of their multigenre work, take time to look as a whole class at the introductions of Jeff Stebbins' "The Allosaurs in Phoenix" (Chapter 9) and/or Amy Wilson's "Finding Strengths in Our Differences" (Chapter 13).

You might let students meet in small groups for exploratory talk before meeting as a whole class. Discuss what the authors are doing with their introductory words. What information are they supplying? What attitude are they establishing?

Try this workshop after students are well into writing their multi-genre papers and have discovered much themselves:

- Ask students to jot down important things readers ought to know before they begin reading their papers. They should reject nothing in this brainstorming and generate many possibilities.
- Team students in pairs. Give each four minutes to talk about the important things he or she jotted. Ask the listening partners to play the role of naturally curious human beings and to "say back" what they understand from the partner's talk. Just as important, instruct them to ask the questions that have risen naturally in their minds. Such questions might lead the writer to reveal more pertinent information that readers ought to know about.
- Take ten or fifteen minutes for everyone to bear down and write directly to prospective readers, telling them things they ought to know before reading.
- Have the class put these drafts aside for two or three days, then come back to them to reread and revise.
- Ask students to determine whether these pieces should preface their multigenre papers.

---

might touch upon a key part of the story. Some multigenre papers need such introductions; some do not.

THE FIRST GENRE

Even more important in orienting the reader with an introduction, however, is the very first genre of the paper. Writers can provide a form and content that foregrounds the information in the multiple genres that follow. Writers might introduce the significant character or describe a crucial setting or central activity. They might introduce a theme that will be carried throughout the paper. They might create an overview of the territory to come. Michael Ondaatje, for example, begins *The Collected Works of Billy the Kid* with a bit of "found" prose and a phantom photograph.

Half of the book's first page is an empty picture frame. Below it are words from L. A. Huffman, the "great Western photographer," as Ondaatje calls him in the credits. Huffman comments on a picture he made of Billy the Kid with the "Perry shutter," the lens wide open. In his comments— which are italicized to indicate these direct quotations—Huffman is more concerned with the detail that the camera was able to capture than with his notorious subject. He calls attention to snowflakes in the air and well-defined wheel spokes. Technology is all for Huffman, not what the technology adds up to. On the following page, however, we learn about the business of guns. Ondaatje creates a stark, blunt poem in the Kid's voice. "These are the killed," the poem begins, "(By me)" and lists the names of men and animals he has killed in his twenty-one years. The second part of the poem repeats the opening line and lists the names of men in the Kid's gang who were killed by Sheriff Pat Garret and his deputies. The final lines read

and Pat Garrett

sliced off my head.
Blood a necklace on me all my life.

As a reader I brace myself—the imagined world ahead will be vengeful, bloody, and matter of fact.

Tone and Topic

My first advisee at Miami University was a tall young woman who stepped into my office, her brow beaded with sweat, a backpack slung over one shoulder, her right hand clutching a bicycle seat. "I'm Nina Barber," she said, setting the seat carefully on the floor and pulling a yellow pad from her backpack. "I've just changed majors," she announced, "and you're my new advisor."

A year later Nina read and wrote, talked, listened, and taught in my English methods class. In her multigenre paper Nina examines with humor and unabashed directness how discomfiting and momentous had been her change in majors from science to English education. In her opener she parodies the form of a typical research project in her former major:

Title: Nina Barber (*Confusitus maximus*)

Abstract: In this experiment we are going to examine how *Confusitus maximus*, common name Nina Barber, reacts to the transition from the world of Science to the world of English. Through this complex morphology, we hope to obtain key information as to the changes that occur in the psyche of the specimen as well as any physical damage to the body due to this change in worlds.

Hypothesis: We will hypothesize that *Confusitus maximus* will come extremely close to a near-death condition due to the trauma that is inflicted upon the specimen. There is only a 2.2% chance that the specimen will actually die. If *Confusitus maximus* does indeed survive, the specimen is hypothesized to adjust quickly to the world of English and, in fact, will eventually find the world of English more desirable than the world of Science.

Methods: By subjecting the specimen to both environments, we first recorded some of the effects that the world of Science had on Nina, beginning at a very young age (see Figure 1). We then collected data from various interactions, writing samples, key observations, and from other outside experts in order to determine the full effect of the change (see Figures 2-7).

Photographs

Jeri Meyer is a fourth-grade language arts teacher in the Mason City School District, north of Cincinnati. As so often happens when students take on the multigenre assignment, Jeri explored a big topic in her life: "those simple, horrible, and wonderful attempts to love" that marked her relationship with her father, a salesman when Jeri was small, frequently on the road, often physically and emotionally unavailable, even when home. Jeri depicts him as a man partly responsible for the hedge of silence that grew between himself and his wife. He nurtured multiple varieties of rose bushes, "a garden of summer sunsets," yet couldn't take sustenance from his wife and two daughters. He contracted cancer, took a mistress, and eventually lost everything: wife, family, the small business he owned, and before his early death, even the mistress.

Jeri's paper is a search for the father she longed to be close to. She relates their story through multiple lenses, expressing bitterness, regret, love, longing, and sympathy in poems, prose poems, letters, song lyrics, narratives, and photographs. She puts together the particulars of her father's life, recognizes his successes, failures, and tragedy, comes, ultimately, to cherish those simple, horrible and wonderful attempts to love.

To foreground the characters involved in the story and the theme of neglect and irreconcilable loss, Jeri opens "finding our way home" with a photograph and two minimalist, metaphorical paragraphs:

> where does it begin? with a small errant seed planted amidst the cabbage and broccoli? with wind born seeds growing too close to tomato vines and pepper plants?

> might it be that it begins with the underestimation of the muscle of weeds? weeds can choke the beauty of delphinium or rose; errant seeds left unattended can invade the soil of the healthiest plants, not to mention what they do to the weakest.

While discussing Jeri's opening, it seems appropriate to tell you how she used photographs through her entire paper to enhance her fine writing. We see her younger sister, her parents, herself, snapshots of her father and mother. "finding our way home" reveals Jeri's long journey in coming to terms with her relationship to her father, in coming to recognize her own adult failings, in shedding most of the bitterness and blame she had felt over the years. She chooses to see the essence that remains, which is love. The last written piece in the paper is a poem in which Jeri renders a visit to the hospital to see her father. He doesn't have long to live, is "waif-like," looking "like a baby bird freshly hatched from shell." He is dying and sometimes delirious, except for "one clear moment of revelation . . . as light floods his face" and he says, "It's so good that we're all back together again." The reader then turns to the last page for one more photograph:

Defining Moment

In *Writing with Passion* (1995) I included a multigenre paper by high school senior Brian McKnight. In a piece titled "The Long and Wonderful Odyssey of the Walrus: A Heart Play," Brian revealed considerable knowledge of his distant teacher, John Lennon. Sensitive and funny, down to earth and hip, Brian is a delight to be around. He is a dedicated and talented actor with a keen sense of drama and a memory for indelible details. He begins his multi-genre paper with a devastating poem of the night the music died:

Unfinished Music #1—John

He hit the pavement
ass-first
Yoko raised
his
head.
He wanted to embrace her
but a hundred people
were
standing on
his arms.
    Oh God, Yoko, I've been shot.

Theme and Topic

I met Kate Boyes while I was teaching at Utah State University. She was the assistant editor of *Western American Literature*. Kate was quiet and accomplished. She took my course, Creative Writing in the Classroom, and wrote a multigenre paper titled "Other Uses" that was, in essence, a chapbook that I hoped she would find a publisher for one day. Her topic was spousal abuse and the slow movement of a woman out from under that Minotaur. Kate's writing was precise and metaphorical, poetic and full of information, chilling and, at the end in a poem titled "Secret Sign," grimly victorious. Finally separated from her husband, the protagonist finds herself next to a woman at a convenience store and notices that "four yellow-green bars mark her upper arm" and knows all too well that the woman also wears "a deep, round thumb print . . . on the soft flesh of her inner arm." The woman starts to cover the bruises but looks into the protagonist's eyes and immediately understands their kinship:

Then slowly, deliberately
she sets down her carton of milk
and rolls up her sleeves.
I push the hair back
from my scarred cheek.
And for a moment we share
without shame
our reflected stigmata.

Kate's writing is palpable and clear-minded. She takes you to the depths of an abusive relationship, merges nightmare and reality, fantasy and history, alcoholism and abuse. Here is the haunting opening piece that sets up Kate's painful, eloquent, and, ultimately, triumphant multigenre paper:

Safe Distance

No body lives
   where I live,
far from jagged edges
   of broken capillaries and the dark
   infusion of blood below the skin,
away from raw nerves
   jutting from the apex of a tooth's
   cracked root deep in the jaw,
nowhere near lavish layers
   of cells smoothed over
   fractured bone shard.
No body lives where I live—
   far
   away
   nowhere
—watching myself from a safe
   distance.

Nothing More Important

Milton White would tell us that our goal when sending a piece to any publication is to get the editor to turn the first page. Good editors, he said, can tell if a piece is going to work after only a few paragraphs, sometimes a sentence, a page at the most.

In writing about the personal essay, Don Murray (1996) discusses the importance of the "lead," a concept he learned forever during his days as a journalist. Murray's urging about the lead applies to the first piece in a multigenre paper as well:

> [T]he lead or first sentence of the essay . . . sets the tone for all that follows. The beginning of the essay should contain—or strongly imply—a central tension (contradiction, irony, surprise, or problem) that will be explored in the essay. The lead is the promise to readers that they and the writer will discover something during the reading that will make them view the world differently from the way they have in the past. (59)

Because multigenre papers are so unconventional, it is crucial that their authors ground readers immediately, orient them to the terrain, establish the central tension. With tongue in cheek Nina sets up the dichotomy between science and English; Jeri works the tension between the happy photo of daughters and father and a garden untended where lost opportunity and unfulfilled love take root; Brian shocks us with the immediate rendering of tragedy that—for awhile—overshadowed John Lennon's accomplishment and our joy in his music; Kate alerts us to the isolation and resignation that accompanies one of the oldest acts of human cruelty.

All this the authors do in their lead pieces, and we readers are not wandering, not bumbling in the dark. Day has broken and we are eager to learn more.

First Piece of the Multigenre Paper

Ask students to create an opening piece that is engaging, informative, and reader-friendly. Robert Cormier says that he likes to grab readers by the lapels in the beginning of his young adult novels. Have students try these options for openers:

- Write a sketch of the central character. Include the significant details of her life, the important characters in it. (You can expand your writing about these details and characters in later genres).
- Write a narrative of your main character performing the central activity of her life. Kamau Brathwaite's "Basic Basie," for example, paints the picture of Count Basie making music at the piano.
- Write vividly about the central image of your topic. In a paper about pitching legend Sachel Paige, you might simply describe in great detail a baseball, a thing he held in his right hand tens of thousands of times. In a paper about Amelia Earhart you might begin by describing the view from the cockpit of her twin-engined Lockheed Electra.
- Find a memorable photo or create a picture that would be compelling for readers to lay eyes on first.
- Develop an extended metaphor that captures your character or topic or theme. Earlier in this chapter, for example, Jeri Meyer wrote about a garden and weeds that choke out good things that might grow in it.
- Render a defining moment in your central character's life. Brian McKnight began with a poem of the shooting of John Lennon. He might have begun with the act of Lennon writing song lyrics or playing with his son or making love to Yoko, all defining moments in his life. Blues vocalist Etta James might be depicted at the microphone on a small stage in a Chicago blues club, her eyes closed, sweat beaded on her brow, singing the blues.

I tell my students that by far the most important part of any piece of writing is the beginning. Those first words, phrases, sentences make or break the piece. Writers have one chance to make a first impression. They need to make a good one that pulls the reader forward.

My allegiance to the lead, however, is fleeting: Once readers have turned the page, those opening words are no longer most important. Once readers are traveling your writing road, other matters loom critically ahead.

8 | TEACHER EXPERTISE
Genre Possibilities

Students can be overwhelmed by the prospect of writing in a multitude of genres. In addition, they might have developed skewed or limited notions about genres. In states where writing proficiency tests are mandatory, enormous pressure comes to bear on students and teachers. When instruction is directed solely to the test, students can come to think that writing is limited to discrete modes of expression: exposition, narration, description (the modes that Ohio requires students to show proficiency in).

The world of writing, though, goes far beyond testing. It is large and contains multitudes. We have fiction and restaurant menus, sonnets and graffiti, recipes and dissertations, love letters and legal documents. In fact, modes of writing are often blended. Narrative needs description. Vivid anecdotes clarify exposition. Fiction can build tension when characters engage in back-and-forth exposition through dialog. Modes mix, genres blend. I'm for teaching an expansive and flexible view of genre.

Evaluating her multigenre project, one graduate student wrote, "A difficult thing for me was trying to think of different genres. Although it sounds juvenile, it would have helped to make a list together of genre possibilities before we began."

No need to feel embarrassed or naive. Such information helps me be a better teacher. You can bet that the next time I taught this graduate course, we spent time identifying genre possibilities.

EXAMINE MULTIGENRE TEXTS

If your students are reading a multigenre novel in preparation to write their own papers, like Avi's *Nothing but the Truth* or Sharon Draper's *Tears of a Tiger*, in addition to discussing meaning be sure to explicitly examine the author's use of genre. Put students in small groups to page through the novel from beginning to end. Identify genres. Make a list of them. Is there a genre the author uses more than once? What might the reason be? Read some of the genres aloud and discuss what the author is able to do, given the possibilities and limitations of the genre or style. If class reading includes multi-genre papers written by students, have the class do a similar analysis of those texts.

BRAINSTORM GENRES, PROVIDE LISTS

Although students might have skewed or limited notions of genre, they also have a good deal of genre knowledge that arises from their youth culture. They will, no doubt, have genres to suggest, like instructions for media components, pieces from teen magazines, liner notes on CDs, music video scripts.

Teachers also should get into the act by teaching students the many genre possibilities they have recognized. Mary Rollinger of Bemus Point High School in New York, for example, supplies her students with a list of nearly three hundred genres, subgenres, and modes of expression, everything from *advertisements* to *yarns*.

MANDATORY CLASSROOM DOING

I hate the expression "to expose" students to something. It sounds clinical and passive, as in exposing children to childhood diseases. It also sounds illicit, as though teachers were giving students secretive glimpses of something by flashing open pedagogical raincoats.

I want more than exposure; I want immersion. I want students to travel the territory of a concept, to get to know its geography. I often engage students in ten or fifteen minutes of writing in a particular genre, subgenre, or writing style at the beginning of a period. Perhaps we will read two or three examples of stream of consciousness from literature or former students. We'll discuss what these authors are doing with language, lapsed punctuation, characters' voice, and sensory impressions. (See Lori Livingston's piece in Chapter 18 and Leah Burge's in Chapter 23.)

I ask students to root around on paper for a few minutes, thinking of characters or situations that might be profitable to render in a stream of consciousness. I'll read another example of the technique to get those language rhythms in the air, then give students ten minutes to try their hands at creating a stream of consciousness. We'll share some of these drafts to show the territory writers have traveled.

GENRE ARISING NATURALLY FROM CLASSROOM WORK

In my ideal English/language arts classroom students are both consumers and producers of all kinds of literature and media. As they read free-verse poetry, they write free-verse poetry. As they read fiction, they write scenes themselves. As they read plays, they render their own dramatic scenes through dialog. I want students to see themselves as writers just as they see themselves as readers.

The more experienced in reading and writing a multitude of genres, the more productive, inventive, and accomplished students will be with their multigenre papers. So for me this assignment works better later in a semester or school year. The more experiential knowledge of genre that students have, the more depth and breadth they can achieve in their papers.

In the best circumstance, when a teacher asks students how they chose genres for their paper, they will answer something like one of my high school students did: "The material I read was so powerful that certain things just grabbed me and I had to write about it. My genres were almost picked for me."

9 | OBSESSION, FACT, AND FANTASY

I've never had a student more captivated with the multigenre paper than Stephanie Musselman. I've accompanied her twice on multigenre journeys—once in high school, once in college. At seventeen Stephanie fell in love with the assignment, investigating the life of Timothy Leary and writing a multigenre paper titled "Give Peace A Chance."

Seven years later Stephanie was my student again in a class at Miami University. She was studying to be an English teacher, and she was eager to write another multigenre paper. I was interested in students pursuing their passions, whether that involved secondary research or investigation into the countryside of the soul. No restrictions. They could write about anything they were passionate about, anything that needed writing. Stephanie wrote a hard-hitting paper full of love, some regret and bitterness, and a little hope about her family, particularly her father, telling his story as a son with an estranged biological father and loving stepfather, a Vietnam veteran, a husband and father, and, finally, a divorcee seeking to find his own balance.

When it came time for Stephanie to student teach the following year in Chuck Tackett's seventh-grade classroom at Ross Middle School in Ohio, she was determined that those preadolescents try their hands at multigenre papers. Mr. Tackett was all for the idea and helped her proceed.

Stephanie began teaching genres with a vengeance. The students learned to write character sketches and personal narratives. She had them experimenting with dialog, stream of consciousness, and free-verse poetry. Jeff Stebbins, whose multigenre paper follows, was one of her seventh graders. When Stephanie and I interviewed Jeff, he explained how baffled he had been by the genre instruction. "Why," he wondered at the time, "is Ms. Musselman teaching all this?" He soon found out.

Jeff had been a self-proclaimed artist for some time. He brought out a book he had written and illustrated in second grade. It was about allosaurs, the dinosaur he was stuck with after someone ahead of him chose tyrannosaurs.

The drawings in the book were colorful, bold, and ferocious. I asked him if he liked to draw better than write.

"I'm a better writer than artist," said Jeff. "I mastered art in sixth grade, since then it's gone downhill. I enjoyed writing everything I wrote in seventh grade. Mr. Tackett made us write a lot. That year was the beginning of the downfall of my artistic career and the upcoming of my writing career."

Stephanie reports that Jeff's paper, "The Allosaurs In Phoenix," was one of the longest produced by her students. After he completed the required genres, he kept on writing, following the evolution of his idea.

"If I decided there was something else I needed to add," said Jeff, "I thought of a genre and put it in."

Those six additional genres earned him extra credit and enabled him to invent a denouement for his story.

Just before our interview ended, Jeff looked across the table to Stephanie, his former student teacher. "You brought it all together," he told her.

So did Jeff.

Table of Contents

48

I chose this topic because I am interested in dinosaurs and science fiction stories.

This story is mostly untrue, but some parts are true such as the charecter sketch, and the encyclepedia article. The allosaurs couldn't eat that much or cause that much damage, but I made it that way to make it more exciting.

I hope that after you read this you may learn a little more about an allosaurus.

This topic is important to me because when I was little I learned so much about dinosaurs, and it would be a shame if all of that information went to waste.

Joe Baker wiped sweat from his brow and sighed.

"Hurry up! We have to clear space for the highway! don't let a cave full of rocks stop you!" He yelled

They carefully set the explosives.

"Double check"! he reminded.

When it was safe they detonated the explosives.

BOOoooommmmmm. As the sound faded away it was drowned out by a louder one.

"HuuuuRRROOOO AAAARRRR,"! the allosaur roared.

"What was that"? Joe asked.

"A cave-in"? a worker mused.

"No, it was something different," Joe said

Then the Dust cleared.

Joe stared.

The Allosaurs

The allosaurs were easily 20 feet tall and 30 feet long. They would have wieghed about three tons, but they were very thin.

One was orange with brown stripes. It was the one that had roared, and it was now sniffing the air contently, sensing food.

The other allosaur was light green freckled, and covered with scars. It was male because it was much smaller. It let out a low growl.

Both allosaurs were lean and hungry, and at the first look weak, but their every movement revealed rippling muscles under their pebbled skin.

We wouldn't have known what the workers fates were if a famous poet hadn't seen it all from the top story of his skyscraper apartment.

He composed a very interesting free verse poem about it.

Until they were gone.

The strong men
blasted the heavy
rock
by the cave.
The Allosaurs
burst out quickly and
blinked in the bright light.
The strong men ran
and the
allosaurs
Followed
and
one
by
one they were
eaten until they
were all gone

Back in the city, Chris Shanhy was walking in an abandoned part of town when he heard a thumping behind him.

He looked back, and saw an allosaurus lumbering towards him.

Running

He turned and ran, and it wasn't far behind, with it's rhythmic Thump, Thump, Thump urging him to run faster but after running for a minute his legs were losing his own running rhythm, because his legs were tired, and he was slowing down, and it was getting closer, and closer, when suddenly the other allosaurus came around the corner, trapping him, and he kneeled down accepting his fate, as both of the allosauruses roared triumphantly.

The Allosaurs ran after a man, chasing and trapping him.
After seeing this the poet wrote a two-voice poem.

Strange prey.

We are Allosaurs	We are Allosaurs
I like to chase	
	I like to eat
This strange new food	This strange new food
They are scared	
	They will run
Then we chase	Then we chase.
It can be fun	It can be fun
But they ar small	
	And I'm still hungry
Lets go find some more	Lets go find some more

The poet ran down the stairs to the bottom floor to go outside. He paused, wondering whether or not he should go outside. He decided that he could write better poems if he went outside. He opened the door and stepped outside

Fear

He looked at his surroundings. There were smashed cars and broken buildings. Glass was all over the streets. He-saw no people

He was shaking with fear and breathing in short sudden gasps. It was almost overwhelming. A hungry male allosaurus stuck it's head out of a window sniffing for him. He turned, legs pumping and ran away screaming, but he had no chance of escaping.

Cameras were rolled into place.

Josh Smith sat across the table from Gayla Archur, a famous reporter.

The Interview started.

Survivor

"We're here-live with Josh Smith, a survivor of the Allosaurus attack. So. Josh, how did you survive"? Gayla asked.

"When the Allosaurus ran towards me I dove into a window. The Allosaurus went running after some other guy," Josh answered.

"And then you got away"? Gayla asked

"Yes although I had to wait another hour before it was safe to come here," Josh stated.

"Thank you for coming, Josh. This has been Gayla Archur for Channel 13 news July 19th, 2000 edition

---

Chad looked at the article he had just written.

It was amazingly good. Chad wasn't surprised. He got up to take it to the editor.

Allosaurus Attack!

Phoenix Enquirer July 10, 2000

It's a horrible scene here in Phoenix AZ. Two Allosauruses were blasted free from a collapsed cave early yesterday morning by an excavation crew that was making room for the new highway. They got to the city at noon. It has been devastating. Buildings have been destroyed. The death count is unknown. The allosgurs are still large and at large, but the national guard and the police have come up with a way to safely capture them

by
Chad Foster

Mary Min looked at the article Chad had written. in the news paper.

"What is an allosaurus"? she asked to herself. She went and got an encyclopedia. When she looked up allosaurus this is what she got.

Allosaurus

Allosaurus - Al·o·sawr·us - A medium sized carnovourous dinosaur.

Allosaurus lived in the Jurassic Period which was part of the Mesozoic Era.

It was 30 feet long and 15-20 feet tall, and wieghed 3 tons.

It's name meant "Different" or Other Lizard", in Latin. It was named that because it had strange bumps over it's eyes.

It was smaller and faster than it's later cousin Tyrannosaurus Rex.

See also! Dinosaurs.

Mary read the article. She was thinking she was reading a section full of stories.

No, it was the front page, and there was a picture, to real to be faked. It also matched the encyclepedia's description, too.

She hoped they could catch it before it killed anyone else.

Harry Wisard saw the allosaurs coming in the distance. He hoped the plan would work.

The cow's mooing was transmitted over a loud speaker.

He chambered a round on his machine gun with a click. He hid behind the cage truck.

Bob Washington was in the cab.

Harry looked at the trapped allosaurs. He taunted them as he jumped into the truck beside Bob.

They started their drive to Washington D.C. were the zoo said they would keep them.

The Zoo's Promise

I hereby declare that I will make sure the allosaurs never get free.

The children would love to see them.

We here At the Washington D.C. Zoo will do everything in our ability to keep them under control

The President has given us permission to hold them.

Thomas Williams   George Heon
Thomas Williams   *George Heon*
President of the   Zoo Directer.
United States of
America

Harry and Bob looked at the document with satisfaction. They could finally dump the roaring Allosaurs.

When the Allosaurs were in the cage, they got and the truck, and drove away.

Allosaurus Expense

# of items	item	cost	total
30	cows	$100	$3,000
60	sheep	$50	$2,500
200	gallons water	$1	$200
500	lbs dog food	$5	$2,500
			$8,200

George looked at the monthly expense. He did some multiplication and figured that if the allosaurs lived 15 years it would cost the zoo $1,476,000. "These things eat a lot of food."

The zoo committee stared at George.

Embaressed, George walked calmly to the door.

It slammed behind him

The committee president, Elizibeth Jones, took over.

"Meeting Adjourned," she said as she ran after George.

Fifty years later a house was demolished.

Former president Thomas Willaim used to live there.

A diary was found in the wreckage. It's last entry started an investigation that lasted twenty more years.

Dear Diary.

July 9th, 2020

Dear Diary,
The allosaurs died today.
Daddy says that when he was president they attacked a city exactly 20 years ago.

Julie Williams

The Allosauruses had died a mysterious 20 years after the attack on Phoenix.

How they survived is and will always be a mystery to us.

10 | TEACHER EXPERTISE
Future Engineers and the Tie-Dyed Set

David Klooster of John Carroll University in Cleveland asked me a question that set me to thinking:

> Are some students better suited to writing multigenre papers than others? Are uptight future engineers as able to succeed with this paper as tie-dyed future artists? Is a more conventional analytical mind as well suited to the multigenre paper as a more associative thinker?

David fingered a truth. Some students take readily to multigenre papers; others have difficulty. From the opening chapter I have maintained that imagination is a way of knowing. Narrative thinking that we find in poems and stories and many other genres often gets short shrift after elementary school. By minimizing, neglecting, or devaluing narrative thinking we penalize students who thrive on it, who need their powers of narrative thinking as they negotiate the world. We should, it seems to me, give such students opportunities to refine and further develop their narrative thinking skills.

At the same time, I want students with more conventional analytical minds to expand their cognitive repertoire and rhetorical skills by gaining further experience with narrative thinking, with knowing the world through story, poem, and song, through imagery, metaphor, and symbol. I want uptight future engineers to learn to use a deft combination of fact and feeling, of the empirical and the imaginative. I want them to understand that truth through analysis and paradigmatic argumentation is but one way of thinking, that equally valid is truth through narrative knowing.

Sirpa Grierson of BYU has addressed this subject, too:

> One interesting discovery that I have made is that some students who have never had "problems" writing required papers struggle with the open-endedness of the multigenre format. Students who like a lot of structure wrestle more with this assignment than do those who consider themselves to be more "creative" types. Scott

confessed: "This format forced me to be creative and also provided me a way to express my creativity that I usually suppress behind a logical, grade-based design . . . . It is hard to know how to attack such an open format."

Such cognitive struggle, I contend, enhances and deepens Scott's intellectual and emotional development. The multigenre paper offers students the opportunity to take part in the production of texts that are driven by narrative thinking, to try out the lenses of poets, fiction writers, playwrights, and artists right in the middle of expository school, long after formal education has turned them toward genres of paradigmatic thought and away from genres that use narrative to think and reveal and experience. One day our students will take jobs in education, auto repair, business, industry, government, manufacturing, sales, law, medicine. No matter what professions they enter, facts and analysis are not enough. If our decisions are to be both sound and humane, we need to understand emotion and circumstance, as well as logic and outcome. Writing in many genres helps minds learn to do that.

11 | TALKING DIALOG

Learning both the music of spoken language and how to use this music are essential parts of the writer's craft.

Ralph Fletcher

One of my university students came back from two weeks of observation in a high school classroom and turned in a paper describing and critiquing the experience. Contained in it was this brief exchange:

Teacher: I see your final copy. Where's the rest?
Student: The rest?
Teacher: Yes, the rest. The other drafts that you wrote before this one.
Student: I didn't write any others.
Teacher: How could you have not written any others? I gave you four class periods to work on them.
Student: I just wrote that one.
Teacher: Here, you need to have another student read this and get feedback. Then you need to revise it . . . twice.
Student: Ah, man, you gotta be kidding. It's gonna be late.
Teacher: You're right, and if you don't finish it, you'll receive an in-school suspension so I suggest you start writing.

Kasie Erlenbach, Junior,
Miami University

In *Writing Fiction: A Guide to Narrative Craft*, Janet Burroway (1987) notes that effective dialog contains "an essential element of conflict. . . . [T]ension and drama are heightened when characters are constantly (in one form or another) saying no to each other" (161). This describes Kasie's teacher and student in spades:

You wrote more than one copy?
No.
You had plenty of time. You certainly wrote more than one copy.
No.
I won't accept this if you have no other drafts. Out of the question.
No, it's too late to do other drafts.
Too bad. I won't accept this as it is, and if you don't do the drafts, I'll suspend you.

In one form or another, no . . . no . . . no . . . no . . . no.

Talking Dialog | **59**

The teacher and student are at odds. The teacher wants students to learn writing processes, apparently wants them to learn the value of revision. The student wants the assignment done. First draft, only draft. They don't engage in small talk. What they say to each other cuts to the core of their different perceptions of school work and writing.

Small talk doesn't contain tension or conflict so you won't find much of it in published writing. This insistence on tension makes dialog perfect for multigenre writers to dive to the heart of matters and reveal conflict, controversy, dilemmas, and opposing viewpoints. Readers get plenty to chew on.

For many years, Tonia tells me, she had a tempestuous relationship with another family member, one that has mended with passing years. Through dialog Tonia imagines the beginning of that relationship:

NEW BEGINNINGS, April 18, 1973, 4:10–4:11

T: OUCH! Hey, what was that?

S: I don't know, but do you mind? It's not very comfortable here with you right on top of me.

T: Well, excuse me! You think I have all the room in the world? Who are you anyway?

S: I'm . . . I'm . . . I don't really know yet, but I think by the way we're being pushed around we're about to find out. Why? Do you know who you are?

T: Duh! Of course I do. I run this joint! I'm the boss.

S: Shh! What's that noise?

T: I dunno . . . hey . . . wait a minute . . . I know that voice. That's the nice lady who sings to me.

S: Oh yeah, I recognize her now, gosh, it sounds like she's having a hard time talking.

T: Yeah, what's she saying? . . . Something about . . . "Get" . . . "Out" . . .

S: What do you think that means?

T: I dunno, maybe you're being evicted.

S: Evicted?

T: Yeah, it's too crowded in here with you anyway, you gotta go.

S: I ain't going nowhere.

T: Oh, yes, you are, I'm bigger than you—don't make me push you out . . . hey, where are you going?

S: Help! I don't wanna go!

T: Hey, how are you doing that?

S: I don't know! I'm being tugged!

T: Well, hurry up, there's a draft!

S: If I go, so do you!

T: I don't think so, pee-wee!

S: Oh, yeah? Well, I've got your leash and I'm not letting go!
T: OH NO! I'm going to get you for this!
S: Yeah, yeah, you can't do nothin'! I'm going to be older than you!
T: We'll see about that, meet me on the outside!

CONGRATULATIONS, TWIN GIRLS!!!!!!!!!!!

Tonia Stacy, Junior,
Miami University

Another student uses dialog to illustrate how culture, idiomatic language, and one-right-answer teaching methods collude to make ESL students feel like fools:

"OH"
(What else can you say when you don't know what you're supposed to know)

Hickory dickory dock, the mouse ran up the _____?
Stairs?
No, it's clock
Why would a mouse run up a clock?
It's just a story. You'll learn
OH

This is hard
It's hard for me too—I'm tearing out my _____?
Pages?
No, hair—I'm frustrated
OH

Wow, we need help. Calling all _____?
Teachers?
No, cars
Why cars?
Not real cars
Fake cars?
No—not cars at all
Why did you call them cars?
That's just the way we say
OH

What else do we say? I need to know
All right, I'll give you some _____?
Stories?
No—pointers
What?
Pointers—I'll point some things out
With your fingers?

No, with my voice
<u>OH</u>

I know it's tough but you've got to pay attention. Take my
_____?
<u>Hand?</u>
No, advice
<u>I need it</u>
I know
<u>OH</u>

Archer Siggers Neal, Junior,
Miami University

DIALOG AMID PROSE—TECHNICAL PROBLEMS

I like dialog exchanges composed simply of the spoken words of participants, like the ones I've shown here. Forget the dialog tags, description, exposition. The writer presents the voices. Readers can tell by the language and its rhythms how the lines should be read, the emotions characters feel, and what they might be hiding by what they aren't saying.

But I also like to see dialog within prose passages, whether fiction or nonfiction. I like the way indented dialog makes a page look. The text seems less daunting with dialog, friendlier to readers. Examining dialog used amid prose can teach students a great deal about the use of dialog tags—or dialog attributions—and the overuse of adverbs.

Take a look at this actual conversation I taped when two high school juniors from a film course came to my room during my planning period to view and talk about the rough cut of the super-8 film they were making. I transcribed our dialog, then added narration and dialog tags:

Tim, Scott, and I watched their film and encountered a huge jump cut in continuity.

"What happened there?"

"I don't know," said Scott. "Doesn't look right."

I reversed the film, then ran the sequence again.

"Oh, Tim gets in the car twice!"

"A little jump cut," I said, "easily fixed. Just cut the least effective shot."

We watched more of the film and suddenly, to my horror, the '57 Chevy roared down a country back road at what looked like 100-plus miles per hour.

"Good Lord!" I said, "I didn't know you guys were doing that! Was that in your script? Didn't I write something about not staging anything dangerous? God, that was fast!"

"That was animated," explained Tim. "You know, the single framing you showed us?"

"That was animated?"

"Yeah, we were only going forty."

"Thank God. I thought, geez, here comes a lawsuit. That's good, guys. That really works. Everybody who comes to our film festival will think I let kids stage high-speed car chases."

Characters speak nine times in that brief scene. Only four times do I use dialog tags to indicate who is speaking. I count on the content of the dialog, the back-and-forth banter of the speakers, and only an occasional dialog tag to keep readers clear about who is talking. The language and punctuation communicate the emotions of the characters.

Notice also that three of the four dialog tags use the word *said*. Beginning writers often do backflips to avoid using this innocuous little word that most readers skip anyway. I understand the gymnastics. We've been taught to avoid repeating the same word in our writing. It sounds bad, often becomes monotonous. With all the best intentions teachers sometimes give kids long lists of words they can use as substitutes for *said*. The results are often hilarious, pulling readers away from the meaning of the dialog and calling attention to the awkward substitution.

Here is the same scene, except this time cluttered with overused and overwritten dialog tags that strain to substitute for *said* and that needlessly interpret how the dialog should be read:

Tim, Scott, and I watched their film and encountered a huge jump cut in continuity.

"What happened there?" I *asked, questioningly*.

"I don't know," Scott *announced, puzzled*. "Doesn't look right."

I reversed the film, then ran the sequence again.

"Oh," Scott *vociferated triumphantly*, "Tim gets in the car twice!"

"A little jump cut," I *soothed*, "easily fixed. Just cut the least effective shot."

We watched more of the film and suddenly, to my horror, the '57 Chevy roared down a country back road at what looked like 100-plus miles per hour.

"Good Lord!" I *exclaimed excitedly*, "I didn't know you guys were doing that! Was that in your script?" I *continued frantically*. "Didn't I write something about not staging anything dangerous? God, that was fast!"

"That was animated," Tim *explained, patiently*. "You know, the single framing you showed us?"

"That was animated?" I *asked incredulously*.

"Yeah," he *comforted, easing my mind*, "we were only going forty."

"Thank God," I *sighed with relief*. "I thought, geez, here comes a lawsuit. That's good, guys. That really works." Then I *added kid-*

dingly, "Everybody who comes to our film festival will think I let kids stage high-speed car chases."

Talking Dialog | **63**

TACKING ON DETAIL

Sometimes inexperienced writers will discover the useful tool of tacking on detail to a dialog tag with a present participial or adverbial phrase:

"It's too late," she said, closing the door.

Tacking on detail is a useful technique but writers must pay attention to what the words literally mean. The tacked-on phrase means that the action contained in it occurs simultaneously with the dialog. A beginning fiction writing student once wrote,

"Ah, I love the smell of the ocean. It's so strong you can taste it," he said as he sucked the air deep within his lungs. Jennifer looked at him and laughed in her shy airy way.

I understand why Jennifer laughed. Try saying the sentences while simultaneously sucking air deep within your lungs.

Even when the dialog and the tacked-on detail can be physically performed together, writers should avoid the habit of tacking detail onto every dialog tag. Here is an absurd example I created to demonstrate the idea to students just before they turned in their stories. After reading this aloud, I gave them a few minutes to edit their dialog:

"Where are you going?" he asked, barring the door.

"To see my lover!" she exclaimed as she picked up the monkey wrench from the dining room table.

"You'll not leave this house tonight," he said, pulling on a football helmet.

"You just wait and see," she said, stepping assuredly toward him.

"No, Samantha, you can't do this!" he said as he flung his arms up to protect himself.

"Get out of my way," said Samantha, moving menacingly toward him, brandishing the monkey wrench with deep malevolence.

"Oh, all right," he said, surrendering and slumping in the nearest chair. "Have your way."

Dialog can fail because of the way it is presented, but surely the main task of a writer is to create dialog that moves and has substance, advances action and reveals character, contains the ring of truth, and creates the illusion of actual speech. In *Technique in Fiction* (1987) Robie Macauley and George

Lanning offer these guidelines for crafting effective dialog. They might be of help to your students:

1. It should be brief, because in life we seldom say more than a few sentences at a time.
2. It should add to the reader's present knowledge.
3. It should omit, or quickly pass over, the routine exchanges of ordinary conversation.
4. It should sound spontaneous but avoid the repetitions of real talk.
5. It should keep the story moving forward; it should not be a mere exhibition of the writer's skill with idiomatic dialog, or of the writer's wit.
6. It should reveal something about the speakers' personalities, both directly and indirectly.
7. It should show relationships among people. (81)

Ralph Fletcher (1996) maintains that "[w]riters are drawn to any real talk that unveils a world: its emotional undercurrents, conflicts, hopes, tensions, and frustration" (41). He further says that "[t]alk is not an isolated element in writing but is tangled up with tension, voice, character, the poetry of surprise (43).

Prompts For Dialog

Ask students to try these ideas for writing dialog.

- Put your central character together with someone significant in his or her life . . . someone loved . . . someone adversarial. Set them to talking about what has passed between them.
- If you are doing research of some biographical figure, put that person together with someone prominent in history either similar or dissimilar. Get them talking about their passions/lifework: Walt Whitman and Emily Dickinson, Eleanor Roosevelt and Hillary Rodham Clinton, Joan of Arc and Adolf Hitler, Bill Gates and Thomas Edison.
- Put the child with the relative she never knew and let them talk out of their own experience.
- Create a dialog that never would have taken place (like Tonia's "New Beginnings") but captures, nevertheless, the essence of the characters' relationship.
- Create a dialog between characters that briefly encapsulates important information.
- Cast the dialog in the form of an interview conducted by the author or another character, fictional or real.

I'll end this chapter with one last dialog. In a multigenre paper that explored her gender, one teacher created this dialog to examine the foundations of patriarchy:

Hallowed Be HER Name

Me: So, you're not who I thought you would be.

God: How's that?

Me: Well, everyone talks about you like you're a man.

God: Uh huh.

Me: I mean, the church leaders are male, all of our prayers are said to *Him*, you know, Our *Father* who art in heaven . . .

God: I get the picture.

Me: And you know, the women in the Bible seem to get second billing. I mean, OK, Mary is pretty revered what with the rosary and earthly appearances, and all, but other than that, there really are no big names.

God: Uh huh . . .

Me: And then you send a man, your son, to save our souls. I mean, why not send a daughter?

God: What exactly is your point?

Me: Why do you give the men all the power? Doesn't it make you angry they keep referring to you as a "He"?

God: Should it?

Me: It would me.

God: Let me ask you a question. Why is gender so important to you?

Me: Because it is important to everyone. It has always been how I've been defined by others. They see a female first, and then they see me—or they can't see me.

God: Well, maybe that is how you see me right now.

Me: So you're not a woman?

God: Why is that important?

Me: Because I would love to be the one to tell the Pope.

Laney Bender Slack, Teacher,
Mason High School

12 | PROSE FICTION

Fiction is fact selected and understood, fiction is fact arranged and charged with purpose.

Thomas Wolfe

When my high school students and I read *The Collected Works of Billy the Kid,* we were intrigued with the Kid's death scene. An omniscient third-person narrator tells the story of Sheriff Pat Garrett and two deputies stopping at a remote ranch one Texas midnight to ask Pete Maxwell where he thinks the Kid is hiding. No one has seen him for three months, not since he killed two guards while escaping jail, where he was awaiting public hanging.

Garrett leaves the deputies outside, enters Pete's hut, wakens the sleeping man, and, crouching by the bed, begins questioning him. Unknown to Maxwell, Billy arrived at the ranch an hour earlier and is drinking with Celsa Guitterrez in the nearby house. On his way to fetch meat for cooking, Billy sees the two men. In Spanish he asks them who they are. When they do not answer, he backs away, wary, and goes to Maxwell's hut. Barefoot and shirtless this hot night, he steps inside the pitch-black room, says, "Quienes son esos hombres afuera, Pete." Here's Ondaatje's tale:

> Garrett recognises the voice. He does the one thing that will save him. Quietly, with his long legs, he climbs over Maxwell's body and gets into bed between Maxwell and the wall. With his rifle in his hands he watches the darkness, trying to make out the shape that is moving towards him. Billy moves over barefoot and asks Pete again. Quienes son esos hombres afuera?
>
> Maxwell doesn't say a word. He can feel Garrett's oiled rifle barrel leaning against his cheek. Billy shakes Maxwell's shoulder and then he hears the other person's breathing. As the only other woman on the ranch, apart from Celsa Guitterrez is Paulita Maxwell—Pete's sister—he doesn't know what to think. Paulita? Pete Maxwell gives a nervous giggle full of fear which Billy mistakes for embarrassment. Paulita! Jesus Christ. He leans forward again and moves his hands down the bed and then feels a man's boots. O my god Pete quien es?
>
> He is beginning to move back a couple of yards in amazement. Garrett is about to burst out laughing so he fires, leaving a powder scar on Maxwell's face that stayed with him all his life. (1984, 92–93)

I shared with students an excerpt from *The Authentic Life of Billy, the Kid* (1980, originally published 1882), Pat Garrett's "true" version of what happened that night:

> It was near midnight and Pete was in bed. I walked to the head of the bed and sat down on it, beside him, near the pillow. I asked him as to the whereabouts of The Kid. He said that The Kid had certainly been about, but he did not know whether he had left or not. At that moment a man sprang quickly in to the door, looking back, and called twice in Spanish, "Who comes there?" No one replied and he came on in. . . . From his step I could perceive he was either barefooted or in his stocking-feet, and held a revolver in his right hand and a butcher knife in his left.
>
> He came directly towards me. Before he reached the bed, I whispered: "Who is it, Pete?" but received no reply for a moment. It struck me that it might be Pete's brother-in-law, Manuel Abreu, who had seen Poe and McKinney, and wanted to know their business. The intruder came close to me, leaned both hands on the bed, his right hand almost touching my knee, and asked, in a low tone:— "Who are they Pete?" —at the same instant Maxwell whispered to me. "That's him!" Simultaneously The Kid must have seen, or felt, the presence of a third person at the head of the bed. He raised quickly his pistol, a self-cocker, within a foot of my breast. Retreating rapidly across the room he cried: "Quien es? Quien es?" (Who's that? Who's that?) All this occurred in a moment. Quickly as possible I drew my revolver and fired, threw my body aside and fired again. The second shot was useless; The Kid fell dead. (128–29)

Ondaatje must have read Garrett's version, we concluded, there were so many similarities in the scenes. We talked about the persona Garrett created for himself in his version: collected and calm, firing in self-defense, relying on keen sensibilities to kill The Kid with the perfect, proverbial shot in the dark. We knew Ondaatje's fictional account wasn't "true." But we wondered how much of Garrett's factual account wasn't either.

One boy said, "So the way Ondaatje wrote about Garrett climbing in bed with Pete, and Billy thinking that Pete's sleeping with his sister, and then thinking, no, he's sleeping with another man, isn't the way it happened?"

"That's right," I said. "That's fiction."

"Well," said the boy, "that's the way it shoulda happened."

I understood the student's disappointment and assertion. The Ondaatje scene of Billy's death had been appealing to him. The nuances and character movements. The irony. The idea of heterosexuality violated. The puzzlement. The giggling and near laughter at such an intense moment. Dramatization, characterization, nuance, and irony are elements fiction does so well. In an intellectually *and* emotionally satisfying way, it reveals truth through fabrication.

In *Smoke Signals* (1998), a film directed by Chris Eyre with writing credit to Sherman Alexie, tribal storyteller Thomas Builds-the-Fire is accused by his traveling companion, Victor, of distorting truth when telling a story about Victor's deceased father. Their new friend, Suzy Song, is confused by this, since she so enjoyed Thomas's storytelling. Thomas asks Suzy to tell a story so that he and Victor can get to know her better.

"Do you want lies," asks Suzy, "or do you want truth?"

"I want both," says Thomas.

So do I. In multigenre papers writers can combine fact with imagination to invent scenes that illustrate truth, or—as Ondaatje did—to render scenes that actually happened but whose details have been lost. Imagination, after all, is a powerful way of knowing, too.

I encourage students not just to report fact in a multitude of genres but also to fictionalize what they cannot know in order to create what could or should have happened. Many students find it hard to do this. Make up? Fabricate? Fictionalize? Isn't that somehow wrong? Like Thomas Builds-the-Fire, won't they be labeled liars? Not necessarily. I don't ask students to fictionalize for purposes of self-aggrandizement (as some critics believe Pat Garrett did). I ask students to try fiction in order to imagine truth, to create a sense of life being lived.

Two Collections of Short Fiction

SHAPARD, ROBERT, and JAMES THOMAS, eds. 1986. *Sudden Fiction: American Short-Short Stories*. Salt Lake City: Peregrine Smith Books.

THOMAS, JAMES, DENISE THOMAS, and TOM HAZUKA. 1992. *Flash Fiction: 72 Very Short Stories*. New York: W. W. Norton.

PERSONA

Everyone who writes creates a persona on the page, an identity for the voice of the writing. Forthright. Dissembling. Smarmy. Glib. Earnest. Trustworthy. Chatty. Laconic. Students have sometimes found it valuable to imagine a fictional persona who reveals information about the multigenre topic.

One of my students created such a persona in her multigenre paper she titled "Young Women Losing Wholeness," her lament for women who have suffered "violence from others or violence to themselves," her chance "to speak out against the larger cultural forces at work killing many of our young women."

Kirsten creates the voice of the mother of an anorexic daughter. The vehicle for this voice is the mother's personal journal entry. Through this genre Kirsten is able to combine what she knows about eating disorders with the deep empathy she has developed toward others. Through the fictional voice in the journal, Kirsten reveals the mother's desperation and helplessness, as well as some terrible details about anorexia.

December 10, 1996

Everything good in Susan is dying. She's not the same child I raised. I raised her to be confident and independent. I thought I had done everything I could to make her independent. I gave her choices, I didn't impose what *I* wanted. I let her make decisions. She's no longer a fun-loving, capable girl. She's a docile creature that wanders home after school, throws her book bag on the kitchen table, flops down on the couch, and speaks to no one. On a good day she'll yell at Ted and me. Yesterday I tried to hug her. She tensed up like I was some evil violator. She shivered, squirmed, and broke free. I'm her mother for Christ's Sake! She will not hug her own mother.

I took Susan to the doctor yesterday. This was her second visit. He pointed out every symptom this child has. How is that going to help her? Does he think he can get her to eat? I know he can't. Susan's cholesterol is 135. He told her that 135 is so low it could trigger a heart attack. Susan didn't seem to care. Actually, her face almost perked up with this news. Does she really just want to die? Something is dangerously wrong here. Susan sat on this cold bench while the doctor poked and prodded. She stared at some diet article pinned on the wall. She had goose bumps making her fur stand to attention. The doctor called her fur "lunago"—a soft woolly hair she had grown to compensate for her loss of fat insulation. I thought to myself, this emaciated body is freezing to death in addition to starving to death. He noted her purplish nails, her swollen ankles, and lifeless hair. She didn't see these things. She *couldn't* see these things.

We didn't speak during the car ride home. She clutched the door handle waiting to bolt from my hostage. Once I put the car in park, she started into the house. I found her standing in the kitchen. Susan was a rod. Her clothes dangled from her as if they were hanging from hangers. I swear she could blow over in a brisk storm. She wouldn't look at me. Instead, she stood over the sink and stared through the window panes. What did she see? She nibbled on dry chicken-broth cubes and took small swigs from a shot of skim milk. She ate 2 cubes instead of the usual 1. Should I mark this as an improvement? Eventually she set her glass aside, snubbed by me, and lingered upstairs. Within minutes, I heard the shower running.

Later in the evening I went upstairs to check on her. I find myself checking on her constantly. I guess I question whether that small body of hers can even sustain life. Her door was shut. I peeked in. The hall light flooded in, illuminating what appeared to be bunched-up covers on her bed. This couldn't be a girl. I didn't know what it was, but it wasn't my daughter.

I went to her bathroom and stood glued to her mirror. What does she see when she looks in this mirror? I couldn't understand. Finally, I knelt down to the shower basin for what had become a daily ritual. I pulled clumps of Susan's blonde, dead hair from the drain, flicking them into the trash. They clung desperately to the side of the can. Something *was* dangerously wrong here.

Kirsten Knodt, Junior,
Miami University

From a fictional stance, Kirsten narrates, describes, informs, persuades, and implicitly argues for us to take action so that anorexic teenagers get the medical and psychiatric help they need to beat their eating disorder.

NARRATIVE SUMMARY VS. DRAMATIC SCENE

At Miami University Milton White wanted his students to go beyond *narrative summary* to create *dramatic scene*. There is a big difference between them, even though each delivers information to readers. Readers will *understand* narrative summary, but they come close to *experiencing* dramatic scene. Dramatic scene is more likely to leave an emotional imprint on a reader. Writers, too, I believe, come to know their topics differently, depending upon how dramatically they write. Look at the narrative summary I've written about an injury my mother once sustained. Information is clearly supplied, but characterization and tension are muted:

> My mother broke the last three fingers of her right hand when she fell on an icy city sidewalk, the bones shattering like peanut brittle. After the bones mended, she began to visit a physical therapist to regain use of the gnarled, stiffened fingers. As the therapist worked with her hand, however, the activity was so painful that she nearly cried. Her usual sense of humor was hard-pressed to assert itself, but when she learned that she'd have to undergo physical therapy twice each day for the next several weeks, it finally emerged.

Contrast that narrative summary with the same information rendered in a dramatic scene:

> The physical therapist sitting opposite my mother pressed steadily on the last three fingers of her right hand. His goal was to touch the stiffened fingers to the palm. With each increase in pressure, Mom leaned farther forward. Those fingers had brushed oil paints onto a thousand canvases, but those fingers were sixty years old when she slipped on an icy city sidewalk. The bones had shattered like peanut brittle.
> Mom leaned forward and her head bumped the therapist's knee. "When do I yell?"

The therapist eased the pressure and grinned. Mom sat up straight, blinking back tears.

"If you want to use the fingers again," he said, "you'll have to do this twice a day."

Mom rolled her eyes. "That'll spice up my life."

A dramatic scene doesn't just inform you about what happens. It sets characters in motion. They do things, they speak, they interact. Dramatic scene appeals to our sense of visual imagery, especially visual imagery that moves. Readers thrive on that.

In a multigenre paper about Mark Twain, a graduate student renders a scene of Twain and his daughters at a carnival. He uses their visit to the House of Mirrors not to explicitly explain the dual identities of Mark Twain but to implicitly reveal them through dialog, description, and drama. During a significant moment, time slows down and life unfolds:

> Ask students to review the prose they have written. If they find narrative summaries, ask them to rewrite them into dramatic scenes.

Outside the tent, the top hatted man with the bullhorn was still calling: "Ladies and Gentlemen. Come see the House of Mirrors. See yourself tall or short, fat or thin. See yourself as your friends see you, as your enemies see you, as your wife or husband sees you . . ."

Inside the tent, rows of bent mirrors lined a worn path from the front flap to the rear. Suzy and Clara ran from one mirror to the next, giggling—the heat didn't seem to bother them. The heat or the musty smell of the yellow canvas. Sam walked behind them, hoping he could lead them outside. Glancing to his side, he watched his neck stretch up like a broomstick from a round body. "You look like a frying pan," Suzy howled.

Sam kept walking, hoping they'd follow, but the girls were still moving from mirror to mirror, giggling. Near the exit, to the left of the path, was a normal mirror. The girls weren't following him. So he roared with pretend laughter—and kept roaring until the two girls ran up to see what was so funny. He pointed at his own reflection and said, "That's the silliest looking thing I've ever seen."

"But, Daddy," Clara said, "that's a *regular* mirror."

Suzy said, "Daddy, you're silly."

Sam guided the girls in the direction of the tent flap. He looked at the mirror again—his head was too large for his scrawny body. Then he looked at the mirror on the opposite side of the path—his head was stretched as big as a hot air balloon. "Mr. Twain," he said to the second mirror, "meet Samuel Clemens."

Scott Brooky, Graduate Student,
Utah State University

Whether your students are doing secondary research and writing multi-genre papers out of that or whether they are exploring aspects of their lives, urge them to use the techniques of fiction. Resist explaining, summing up, and analyzing. Create scenes instead. Become like the novelist or filmmaker. Dramatize without interpretation. Make setting and character vivid with detail and nuance. Invent dialog. Use active verbs. Such writing will not only make for engaging reading; it will make for engaging writing.

13 | LEARNING WHAT WE NEED

We write to expose the unexposed. If there is one door in the castle you have been told not to go through, you must. Otherwise, you'll just be rearranging furniture in rooms you've already been in. Most human beings are dedicated to keeping that one door shut. But the writer's job is to see what's behind it, to see the bleak unspeakable stuff, and to turn the unspeakable into words—not just into any words but if we can, into rhythm and blues.

Anne Lamott

Amy Wilson—now a middle school teacher—was a college junior when she went to an urban high school for two weeks of observation and interaction with students. What she experienced altered her education. For her multi-genre paper she had planned to research and write about the education of girls. But after the school visit, she had something new to investigate.

In "Finding Strengths in Our Differences" Amy combines research and experience to imagine a pedagogy that blends writing instruction with an egalitarian, multicultural philosophy. Because of the many voices Amy creates and the dramatic nature of the paper, presenting "Finding Strengths in Our Differences" as readers' theater breathes life into the multigenre concept. I've used the paper in this way in dozens of classes and workshops. One teacher who saw Amy's paper performed wrote to me about the experience:

> Amy clearly found a personal learning agenda in issues of multi-cultural understanding and lack of understanding as well as the institutional racism or "cultural habits" that influence human in-teractions. I was enormously impressed with her capacity to craft a lot of fiction including dialogue between teachers—and between teachers and students, and also to craft poetry read by and written by students.
>
> Esther Gray,
> Illinois State University

Amy's paper isn't an expository essay. It isn't a discursive argument with an explicit thesis about issues of multiculturalism, racial intolerance, and the teaching of writing. "Finding Strengths in Our Differences" is a multigenre paper that *dramatizes* different voices with different views, some that oppose each other ideologically.

What so troubled Amy during the school observation and sparked her multigenre project was a student's racist, inflammatory writing. Because she didn't know how to handle the situation, she felt like a failure as a teacher and citizen interested in social justice.

The content of "Finding Strengths in Our Differences" is troubling and urgent. In addition to immersing yourself and your students in the issue and discussing it, be sure to take note of Amy's implementation of the multi-genre format:

- her conversational introductory letter to the reader—in this case, me—that explains the paper's context and her inspiration to write it
- her enlightening "End Notes" that reveal information about her writing processes and research
- her imaginative skills in creating a cast of characters, including a persona for herself
- her skill in creating distinctive voices—some of whom say things we'd rather not hear—and the deftness with which she weaves these voices together, literally so in her persona's final monolog.

Amy has a strong sense of theater. As a child and high school student she acted in dramatic productions. And as a communication education major at Miami she took several theater courses. "When I wrote this paper," says Amy, "I visualized it as if it were a play. That made it easier to write."

December 15, 1995

Dear Dr. Romano:

I can't believe the multigenre paper is done! Wow, what an experience completing it. At times, I thought I'd never see this point. It's a nice feeling though; I really *enjoyed* my topic and I had a strong connection to it. My topic, to refresh your memory, is encouraging multiculturalism in writing, in addition to dealing with racial tension and the "contact zone." I had such a strong connection because the idea for my paper basically came from the first field experience—when one of my students, Sarah, asked for help with a controversial paper. I didn't know how to handle race in writing, especially racial prejudice. I have a much better idea of how to deal with it now and how to prevent it in student writing—by encouraging multiculturalism in writing from day one.

I wish I could have been more diverse in my topic, but unfortunately, I seemed to concentrate on the "black/white" aspect. It is the aspect of multiculturalism that I am most familiar with and connected to. My interest isn't just restricted to one kind of culture;

in fact, I learned that there are many different cultures (the "A list" and "B list"), and an effort should be made to focus on those cultures—it can only enrich the student.

My paper is set up to show a teacher (Janice Morgen) trying to encourage multiculturalism in her students' writing. It isn't easy, and the struggle is shown to come full circle—the paper starts with her questioning how to encourage multiculturalism and it ends with her questioning how to deal with the "contact zone." This shows that we still have a lot to learn, practice, and perfect in this area.

One final note: the bibliography features some articles that I didn't directly refer to in the end note page. I used these sources just as background information, to help as a "springboard" for other ideas.

Thank you for looking at my work. I feel very proud of this project and it's probably one of the most important things I've worked on at Miami. I hope you enjoy it!

Sincerely,

Amy Morgen Wilson

FINDING STRENGTHS IN OUR DIFFERENCES: ENCOURAGING MULTICULTURALISM IN WRITING

Amy Morgen Wilson, Miami University

A Dilemma

I pass by Sarah's desk.

"Help me write this," Sarah says.

I kneel down to desk level and peruse her paper. "Okay, Sarah, where do you need help?"

Sarah begins to break it down. "Does this make sense?" she asks.

> Change of heart . . . I'm trying to describe . . . the black protest . . . I used to be one of the most non-prejudiced people . . . I've totally changed . . . the black students . . . my boyfriend went to get his gun . . . THEY'RE so obnoxious . . . black, black, black . . .

My head swells. FOCUS!!!! Okay, how do I deal—

Try to concentrate on the paper itself, but what about its content??? I can't ignore it and just look for missing commas . . .

Why, Sarah? Don't start this kind of feeling now, Sarah.
Keep writing, Sarah. God, you're too young for this.
Keep writing, Sarah.

ASSIGNMENT: fourth period—Due 9/17

Write a poem about you—anything goes!

Sense

Open your eyes—LOOK at me.
No, don't just see me, fool
LOOK at me.

LOOK at my skin
Ya, it's dark, much darker than yours.
It's not a nice honey brown
Mine's thick chocolate, honey.

Open your ears—LISTEN to me.
No, don't just hear me, damnit
LISTEN to me.

My voice is sometimes loud and
obnoxious, I know that.
My words are round and unsharpened—
we only understand ourselves ya'll say

FEEL my hair, fool don't
touch it
FEEL my hair.

Coarse, curly, greasy, ya say,
greasy from relaxer
My hair grows as I did—
harsh, unruly, but thick and full.

Come closer, there's more!
TOUCH me, LISTEN to me, SEE me
Then, po' fool, you'll know me.

Tanesha, Grade 11

For the Record:

TEACHING JOURNAL, 9/18

I had no idea Tanesha would write something like this. I mean, what teacher would expect it when she assigns a simple poem about "yourself." I expected the usual—I'm tall, I'm athletic, I love my cat, I'm going to be rich and famous. I know I said, "Anything goes," but this is real, it's rough. Bravo, Tanesha! Risk-taking at its finest. I'm mildly impressed with the poem itself—rather simple free-verse form, almost sing-songy. I like its off-rhythm. There's something deeper, though. And I'm afraid to *feel* it as Tanesha says. I am so happy she wrote about her "blackness"—that took guts. But how do I handle it? Identifying herself with her race is strong and in-your-face, but is it too in-your-face? I mean, with the new trend—a unified classroom, we're different but the same, multiculturalism, melting pot—how do I handle this outright declaration of Tanesha's "black pride," her black identity? This assignment asked for it, and I wasn't ready to handle this whole greater issue. Race and writing: should it or can it work? Simple. A poem about you—anything goes. Are my students trying to tell me something?

Barb's Dirty Ashtray

TEACHER'S LOUNGE 3:34 P.M.

"So, Janice, what's on your mind, sweetie?" Barb crushed out the stub of her cigarette. "Don't think I'm prying but after twenty-some years I know a frustrated teacher when I see one." She grabbed another Marlboro Light from the pack lying next to Janice's sprawled papers.

"Oh, really, it's nothing," Janice replied, peering above her glasses, meeting Barb's glance across the table. "Well, maybe it is . . . okay, tell me what you think."

"Shoot, honey."

"I've been doing some thinking about the writing done in my class. I mean, I've been happy for the past three years with the same kinds of topics and assignments, but I feel that my kids need something they can sink their teeth into, something more than just "describe your room . . . who's your hero in your family." I see a greater need, especially with the diversity in our student population lately. Our school is getting to be a real melting pot and I want my students' writing to reflect that, too. Any suggestions?"

Barb took a long drag and blew a line of smoke as she looked up to the ceiling at an invisible answer. After a long pause, she said, "Honestly, honey, after all this time in this profession, I haven't had the energy or time to even worry about this multicultural, melting pot shit. I don't see a need for us to change the way we teach just because our school is goin' down the tubes." Barb began coughing and practically hacked up a lung.

She recovered and continued, "I applaud your efforts, but when you get to my age and reality hits you in the face a couple times, you'll understand that no matter what you do, those colored and Hispanics and other immigrants just don't write and learn well—they're always remedial. That excludes those Orientals, of course, they know everything. But breaking your back to come up with 'diverse' writing assignments will only go so far. Those colored kids will still speak their mumbo-jumbo lingo in class and in the halls. Can't understand a word."

"So I take it you have no suggestions to offer—thanks anyway."

Janice adjusted her glasses and went back to reading her papers. Barb blew out another cloud while she crushed out another cigarette.

Bulletin

Missing: One bright, energetic, open-minded English teacher. Characterized by wide blue eyes that droop when tired, a younger-than-her-age appearance, and a new desire to fit multiculturalism into her students' writing.

Last Spotted: Sunday, 11:00 a.m., pouring over books and journals at a corner table in the public library . . .

Janice's Mental Notes:

11:38 A.M. SUNDAY—BANNER PUBLIC LIBRARY

Okay, *English Journal*, old trusted source. Let's see, good article even though it's geared to multiculturalism in literature. Wow—great definition—yes, that's it!

> We know from our own experience that there is no such thing as monoculturalism. There is only multiculturalism, for each of us, for all of us. (Fishman, 75)

> Rita Dove, the current U.S. poet laureate, addresses just this complexity. "There are times when I am a black woman who happens to be a poet," she said, "and times when I am a poet who happens to be black." (75)

Tanesha's poem. This makes sense—and I didn't even know our poet laureate was a black woman. And she doesn't define herself as truly one "thing." That's important. Oh, here, even more . . .

Pluralism assumes that:

1. Students and those immediately around them represent multiple cultures individually as well as collectively;
2. Students can learn about their immediate cultural plurality to begin developing an inclusive cultural/multicultural perspective;
3. This recognition of multiple cultures in their own lives can help students understand multiple cultures further removed from their own. (76)

Okay, I like this. Not too out-of-touch, possible to incorporate into writing assignments. Pluralism, pretty cool—I can deal with that.

And here's what I need to guide me—definitions of what "culture" is. Oh, joyous day!

The "A" List: Race, Nationality, Ethnicity, Religion, Gender
The "B" List: Class, Age, Geography, Education, Occupation,
                Family Status, and Sexual Orientation (77)

Now, I'm getting somewhere (without raspy Barb blowing smoke
in my face) . . .
Another EJ—responding to multicultural literature . . .

Students were assigned journal topics, in which they had to
write in the persona of one of the novel's characters, and
wrote letters to each other "in role" . . . (Dyer, 79)

Great idea! Maybe it could be letters to a character in a poem or
they write as a significant person in history—a person of a different
race/culture/gender than theirs. But is that too risky? Put that one
on the back burner.
Here's food for thought—

We know that the natural feelings of discomfort we experience around those whose appearance or practices or beliefs
are different from ours can lead to distrust, hostility, and
even hatred . . . . The only available remedy is education.
(Brandt, 3)

Speaking of food—I'm hungry. I need some lunch and I gotta
get out of this library!

Tuesday Morning, Fourth Period—
Poetry Discussion

Ms. (Janice) Morgen: So who would like to read the next poem on our
handout? [Looks around room at raised hands]
Okay, Jason, why don't you give it a shot?

Jason: [Reads] I play it cool—

Ms. Morgen: Jason, don't forget, always say the title and author
when reading a poem out loud. Okay, sorry to in-
terrupt, try again.

Jason:

"Motto" by Langston Hughes

I play it cool
And dig all jive.
That's the reason
I stay alive.

My motto,
As I live and learn
        is:
*Dig and be dug
In return.*

[some laughter]

Ms. Morgen:	So what do you think? Why the laughter?
Eric:	Well, I don't know 'bout everybody else, but it sounds pretty outdated to me—I mean DIG and JIVE? C'mon, this must've been written in the sixties, right?
Jenny:	It's a hippie poem, right, Ms. Morgen?
Ms. Morgen:	Close, Jenn. Why did you say that, though?
Jenny:	I don't know, 'cause that's how hippies would sound. They'd say those things, right?
Ms. Morgen:	Exactly! Did everyone hear what Jenny said?
Josh:	[jumping right in] So it is a hippie poem!
Ms. Morgen:	Not quite what I was referring to, Josh—but thanks for the enthusiasm! Actually, Jenny was right on the money when she said, "That's how they sound, they'd say those things." That's the one thing this little poem has—a lot of voice! Each one of us has our own particular "voice" that characterizes who we are.
Tara:	That's sort of what you graded us on for that one journal entry.
Ms. Morgen:	Right, so you all are pretty familiar with the idea. But a lot of people don't know that a writer's voice can be greatly influenced by his or her culture. So even though this sounds like a hippie—which is a kind of "culture" in itself—what else does the voice in the poem sound like?
Jason:	When I read it, it sounded like a rap, so I guess Langston Hughes could be black.
Latrice:	Ya, that's the way black folks talk—not any more. I'd get laughed at if I talked like that—but I can tell a brother wrote this poem.
Ms. Morgen:	Very good, Jason and Latrice. Latrice, you identified with this poem because it's a part of your culture. Do you think other students could enjoy and identify with this poem even if they aren't black?
Katie:	Well, I'm not black but I like rap music. I listen to it a lot because I like the heavy bass and rhythm—it's just who I am.
Ms. Morgen:	Excellent, Katie! It's just who you are. I like that! That's one of the things I want you guys to remember from this discussion—just because a black poet writes in a black voice, same with Latino, or Asian, or whatever, that doesn't mean you can't enjoy certain aspects and identify with it if you're of another culture or race. Yes, Latrice?
Latrice:	Isn't there another one like that "Motto" poem, umm, by, I think its like Gwen Brooks or something? I can't really remember all of it but it sort of goes like "We real cool, we left school, we jazz June, something something something." I like it 'cause it's real jazzy and simple.
Ms. Morgen:	Wow, Latrice, great comparison of styles. I didn't even think of that one. Latrice's referring to Gwendolyn Brooks's poem

"We Real Cool." She's another black poet. Speaking of which, Sarah, why don't you read our next poem, "Cotton Song."

Sarah: Okay.

"Cotton Song" by Jean Toomer

Come, brother, come. Lets lift it;
Come now, hewit! roll away!
Shackles fall upon the Judgment Day
But lets not wait for it.

God's body's got a soul,
Bodies like to roll the soul,
Cant blame God if we dont roll,
Come, brother, roll, roll!

Cotton bales are the fleecy way
Weary sinner's bare feet trod,
Softly, softly to the throne of God,
"We aint agwine t wait until th Judgment Day!

Nassur; nassur,
Hump.
Eoho, eoho, roll away!
We aint agwine t wait until th Judgment Day!"

God's body's got a soul,
Bodies like to roll the soul,
Cant blame God if we dont roll,
Come, brother, roll, roll!

Ms. Morgen: Great job, Sarah. That's got some tough dialect in it. But what does that dialect indicate?

Tanesha: That this poem takes place in the South—I get the feeling it's about the slaves and plantation life.

Ms. Morgen: Right you are, Tanesha. This poet, Jean Toomer, wrote a lot about the South and the black way of life in the South. He wrote very beautiful poetry and prose that was rather innovative—that's why this one may be a little more confusing. Right now, I want you all to take ten minutes and write your reaction to this poem. Keep in mind the different style of "Cotton Song" compared to "Motto"—Toomer's poem has all the elements of a Negro spiritual, while Hughes' poem has the elements of a rap. Write your reactions to "Cotton Song," just like our discussion of "Motto." Great discussion, by the way.

ASSIGNMENT: Due 11/3

Write a hypothetical letter to the President of the United States discussing the problem of racial/cultural intolerance in our country. What can be done to remedy the problem? What should the President do? What changes would you like to see or should things stay the same? Be specific and concentrate on a few main issues. Be brave and really probe into the issue of multiculturalism/cultural intolerance. Express your ideas!

LETTER TO THE PRESIDENT

Jeremy H. Gallagher
November 3

Dear Mr. President,

I have a few things to say about the issue of racial intolerance. I'm sure this is a topic you hear a lot about so you're probably sick of it. Don't worry, I know you have a lot to do, so I'll make this short.

I am an eleventh grader and almost ready to go out into the "real world" (whatever that is). I'm fearing this—not because of my youth and inexperience—but because of the people in this country and this world that are making this a horrible place to live. I'm sure you have a similar fear. Mr. President, I realize this country is suppose to be the "melting pot," but I'd rather not be melted with queers, colored people, and illegal aliens. I feel that I'm happy with the way I am, why do I want anything to do with them? Let's face it: Blacks are dummer than whites—it's been proven with I.Q. tests—and that's why they stay poor and turn to crime and have tons of babies that we end up paying for. Hispanics are just trying to sponge off the hard workers like my dad and every one crossing the border illegally should be shot or sent back, and queers should *all* be shot—they don't fit in our society. My views reflect a lot of thought on my part, it'd be nice to make everyone get along, but some people don't belong in this country—they just make it worse.

That's why I don't believe racial intolerance is bad—it's necessary for our country to survive. Whites (who are straight) need to keep the power of this country like Congress and the Supreme Court. As long as that power still exists, we won't have problems with racial intolerance.

Sincerely,

Jeremy H. Gallagher

Barb's Unwelcome Thoughts
TEACHER'S LOUNGE 3:10 P.M.

"So, Janice, honey, what's up with this controversial letter Jeremy Gallagher wrote for your class? That kid's a weird one anyhow, too quiet I always said. Dish the dirt, sweetie!" Barb blew a line of smoke in Janice's direction.

"Don't worry, Barb. I'm handling it just fine on my own. Really, I need to work on what I'm writing here, if you don't mind." Janice fanned the air in front of her and started writing again.

"Janice, hon, you know what I told you when you first wanted to start with the multicultural shit. Word spreads quick around here. I heard you haven't even dealt with him yet. If you want my advice, I tell ya—just dismiss the letter, tell Jeremy that you can't deal with that kind of writing, give him a 'C' and brush it off. Don't worry, honey. This is what happens when you dive into the sticky stuff like race and culture. Go back to your safe topics, I tell ya—"

"Barb, thanks for your advice, but I don't need it. I really need to get back to my writing now . . ."

Oh Boy.

TEACHING JOURNAL, 11/5

Janice, what have you gotten yourself into? God strike me dead for saying this but maybe I should've listened to Barb—stick with the safe topics, sweetie! No, how could I do that when students like Tanesha are inspiring me to do better? [Tanesha speaks] *Pay attention to our cultural voices!* Inspire those cultural voices!

I felt like I was actually starting to do that and SUCCEEDING at it! I was getting some great stuff from the students—I think they felt at ease expressing themselves culturally and then also, they felt at ease discovering other cultures through writing. They were making connections—to their own writing and to famous writing. Then this—I just thought I'd push them a little further. I didn't think I'd get something tough to deal with. Jeremy's piece really scares me—[Jeremy speaks] *queers should all be shot*—how do I handle it without hurting his writing? It surprises me, he's one of my best.

This is exactly what I was reading about in the library—the thing called the "contact zone." In one respect, I like the idea of Miller's article—"putting ideas and identities on the line" and grappling with tough issues in the classroom. The only problem is, I wasn't prepared for it to be in my face, in the form of some pretty hateful words. Jeremy is right in his letter: [Jeremy speaks] *we shouldn't be in the melting pot.* We should retain our cultural identities, but learn about others, learn how to deal with them. He's not dealing with them, he's resisting in a harsh way that I don't agree with. Those words aren't acceptable in my class. I want to work through this letter with him, [Janice and Jeremy speak together] *but it will be difficult since I disagree with his/her views.*

Most importantly, I don't want him, or any student to stop writing. Especially when their writing deals with issues like race and culture—these issues NEED to be written about! Maybe I'll have him rewrite the letter from a gay person's point of view. Maybe I'll conference with him. Maybe . . . I don't know. Now that I've gotten to this point, how do I deal with this completely different level of the "contact zone"?

Here's a quote I like:

> We need to find ways of urging writers not simply to defend the cultures into which they were born but to imagine new public spheres which they would like to have a hand in making. (Harris, 41)

End Notes

PIECE #1: A DILEMMA

This piece was written as a result of my field experience. I encountered a student named Sarah who had a controversial piece like the one the character is describing. Just like Janice, I was faced with the initial shock of "how do I deal with this?"

PIECE #2: SENSE

This piece was inspired by Chapter One of Donald L. Rubin's book *Composing Social Identity in Written Language*. In this chapter, a similar assignment was given to a class and a black student chose to write about himself as a "black man." I also received some help and inspiration from another field experience student (she gave me inspiration with her use of black dialect, like "po' fool," to make poetry "decorated with culture") and from my African American friend at Miami, Kristina (she gave me some help cleaning it up).

PIECE #4: BARB'S DIRTY ASHTRAY

Some of this dialogue was influenced by my own high school experience, in which our school became significantly "diverse" as I completed my years. Also, some of Barb's negative opinions came from the article "Basic Writing: Pushing Against Racism," by William Jones.

PIECE #5: JANICE'S LIBRARY TRIP

This piece features the research Janice did in order to learn more about multiculturalism in writing—since Barb wasn't a big help. Janice's findings and thoughts mirror mine as I went through everything. Citations made in the piece, refer to bibliography.

This piece was greatly influenced by the article "Black Poetry: Versatility of Voice," by Mitchell and Henderson. I thought it was great how it made black poetry seem more universal, not so "scary" to those who may be timid to use it in their classes. Some inspiring words in this one. I used the poem "Motto" by Langston Hughes and "We Real Cool" by Gwendolyn Brooks, both found on page twenty-three. In addition, I used *Cane* by Jean Toomer for the poem "Cotton Song," found on page nine.

PIECE #7: LETTER TO THE PRESIDENT

This piece is written in Jeremy's style—an eleventh grader—so any mistakes are deliberate. I was influenced by the overall tone of Miller's article "Fault Lines in the Contact Zone." Miller's description of the controversial paper gave me the basis to write one of "my own." I tried to make Jeremy a little more thoughtful about it, though. Also, a lot of the stereotypes that Jeremy used came from the article "The Stereotype Within" by Marc Elrich.

PIECE #8: BARB'S UNWELCOME THOUGHTS/JANICE'S JOURNAL ENTRY

First, we get to deal with Barb again! This time, I was influenced by Miller's description of the reaction to AT&T's magazine scandal. In the article, Miller argued that the usual reaction to something controversial in the "contact zone" is to label it a disgrace, an error, and toss it aside. Barb follows that philosophy and advises Janice to not deal with Jeremy's letter head on. Of course, Janice knows better.

In Janice's journal entry, she reflects on the two articles she read about the contact zone, Miller's and "Negotiating the Contact Zone" by Joseph Harris. She seems overwhelmed by the situation and it leaves her questioning what to do, just like she did in the beginning. The final quote comes from page forty-one of the Harris article.

Bibliography

BRANDT, RON. 1994. "Overview: Differences That Divide, Values That Unite." *Educational Leadership* 8, 3.

DYER, BRENDA. 1995. "Write the Vision: Teaching Multicultural Literature from a Global Perspective." *English Journal* 84, 78–81.

ELRICH, MARC. 1994. "The Stereotype Within." *Educational Leadership* 8, 12–15.

FISHMAN, ANDREA R. 1995. "Finding Ways In: Redefining Multicultural Literature." *English Journal* 84, 73–79.

HARRIS, JOSEPH. 1995. "Negotiating the Contact Zone." *Journal of Basic Writing* 14, 27–42.

HUGHES, LANGSTON. 1996. "Motto." *The Collected Poems of Langston Hughes.* Edited by Arnold Rampersad. New York: Alfred A. Knopf.

JONES, WILLIAM. 1993. "Basic Writing: Pushing Against Racism." *Journal of Basic Writing* 12, 72–80.

KRIM, NANCY, and SANDRA EARLE WORSHAM. 1993. "Team-Teaching Long Distance: Making Connections Across the Mason-Dixon Line." *English Journal* 82, 16–23.

MILLER, RICHARD E. 1994. "Fault Lines in the Contact Zone." *College English* 56, 389–408.

MITCHELL, ARLENE HARRIS, and DARWIN L. HENDERSON. 1990. "Black Poetry: Versatility of Voice." *English Journal* 79, 23–28.

RUBIN, DONALD L. 1995. *Composing Social Identity in Written Language.* Hillside, NJ: Lawrence Erlbaum Associates.

TOOMER, JEAN. 1973. *Cane.* New York: Liveright.

VAN AUSDALL, BARBARA WASS. 1994. "Books Offer Entry into Understanding Cultures." *Educational Leadership* 8, 32–35.

14 | WHAT OF TRADITIONAL RESEARCH PAPERS?

High school teacher Melinda Putz cites a severe limitation of the multigenre paper: "Students do not learn to carry on a sustained written discussion of a topic."

There is, of course, nothing to rule out students including in their papers of multiple genres incisive, expository discussion or revelatory analysis. My students, however, have rarely done this. My hunch is that they have been required to write in standard expository ways for so many years that given this multigenre opportunity they flee toward the freedoms of narrative genres and away from what they see as the strictures of paradigmatic ones.

But learning to carry on sustained written discourse is certainly a skill we want students to develop. They will need to be able to do this in college and in countless jobs they might take in the future. Any number of circumstances in their lives will call upon them to make a reasoned and logical case.

David Klooster, a teacher at John Carroll University, drives to the heart of this matter:

> How do we describe the advantages, the suitability of the multigenre paper in writing courses that serve the curricular purpose of preparing students to read and write in other courses across the curriculum? Do we mislead students to think that the multigenre paper will serve them in most academic contexts?

No doubt in my mind that we mislead students if we do not make part of multigenre work serious discussions of purpose, audience, and power.

> What is the writer's purpose?
> Who will read the multigenre paper?
> Who will judge, evaluate, and grade the paper?
> What does the judge/evaluator/grader value?

If the student cares about the final grade—if the writer cares about publication—answers to those questions are crucial. Is the teacher *inviting* multigenre papers, as are the teachers I have quoted in this book? If the teacher isn't inviting such writing, would he or she be open to multigenre papers? Could a multigenre response to an assignment be negotiated?

We never know the answers until we ask these questions. Even though I hear many stories of teachers who accept only strictly defined expository writing, I also know stories of writers—students and adults both—and of editors who have stretched the envelope of "appropriate" styles of writing. In the February 1998 issue of *English Journal*, for example, editor Leila Chris-

---

The Dilemma of Plagiarism

In traditional research papers students create expository prose to carry information they have gathered from expository prose. Intentional and unintentional plagiarism can occur without much effort or duplicity on students' part. Not so with multigenre papers. Expository passages don't fit easily—unacknowledged—into the flow of a paper that combines imagination and multiple genres. "The opportunity for plagiarizing or major rewording is no longer available," writes Karen Blanchette.

The use of multiple genres, though, can invite plagiarism of another sort. "Difficulties arise," notes Kris Naftel, "when students pull from other sources and neglect to try their own hand at writing various genres. The Internet offers numerous temptations/choices. Output is immediate."

Melinda Putz seemed almost nonplused in describing one incident of plagiarism: "Incredibly, some students had trouble with the Internet; they didn't know if it should be used as a source or as original material. One student, for example, included in his paper journal entries by members of a rock group, counting them as *his* pieces of writing."

Teaching scholarly and creative responsibility is a challenge we must meet head-on and discuss frankly with students, showing them ways to incorporate source material into their papers with efficiency, accuracy, and honor. After all, we want students to learn to gather ideas and information from other sources and then to build their own writing from them. The topic of plagiarism is worth mini-lessons, discussion, and practice in documenting sources, preparing informative end notes, translating researched facts into imaginative genres.

Amy Wilson's "Finding Strengths in Our Differences" (Chapter 13) is an excellent model in this regard. Have your students deconstruct what Amy has done. She combines creativity and scholarly responsibility. She imagines, she quotes sources, she includes the creative and scholarly work of others. And she does this all with responsibility, clarity, and candor. Her "End Notes" reveal how research and imagination combined in her to make art.

tenbury published a multigenre article—its first, to my knowledge—by John Gaughan, "From Comfort Zone to Contact Zone." In April of 1999 co-editors Maureen Barbieri and Linda Rief of *Voices from the Middle* published a multi-genre article by a student teacher, Sara Boose—the first time, to my knowledge, that that journal has used such a piece.

But I'm not advocating that multigenre become the sole mode of writing throughout the curriculum. I do see it, however, as an important part of every student's development as a writer and thinker.

Melinda's and David's concerns relate to a larger issue, though, especially in high school and college: What of the traditional research paper? The compelling paradigmatic voice. The voice that argues and illustrates and extends thinking in a logical progression of language and ideas. The voice that understands the power of thesis statements and knows to incorporate powerful secondary sources.

Though norms of writing and publishing evolve and stretch, many of us are responsible for teaching traditional research paper format. High school teacher Nanci Bush acknowledged that this was her biggest concern about diving into the realm of multigenre. She addressed the dilemma by requiring students to write a traditional research paper earlier in the year. Mary Rollinger requires that somewhere in their multigenre work students include a succinct thesis statement.

Alys Culhane of Plymouth State College sees her work with students writing multigenre papers as compatible with her obligation to teach research skills.

In doing multigenre/I-search papers, students do develop the research skills needed for academic writing. For example, my students have to do three personal interviews, and come up with four print and four Internet sources. They have to share ideas with one another, and also do extensive revision of their work-in-progress. As for this business of thesis-driven writing, my usual response is, in most cases, that the thesis in multigenre, I-search type writing is implicit. My job is to point this out to students, so that they will recognize that this too is a valid way of communicating ideas to others . . . . As I see it, one of my jobs is to get the academic community to think in broader terms about what constitutes good academic writing.

15 | THE MANY WAYS OF POEMS

Poetry is the bouillon cube of literature.
Donald M. Murray

One term my English methods students read Paul Janeczko's *Poetspeak: In Their Work, About Their Work* (1983). Students were to come to class with a "one-pager," a typed, single-spaced, one-page response to their reading. Rebekah Murcray's lead startled me and pulled me in: "Ever since seventh grade I have lived in mortal fear of poetry."

Rebekah went on to describe experiences with poetry that had made her jittery and fearful. She started with having to memorize a Robert Frost poem that was two pages long, then recite it before the class, summarize it, and tell about the poet. Rebekah kept confusing the order of the stanzas and ended up with the only failing grade in her "entire schooling career."

In another class Rebekah spent ten weeks learning the ins and outs of Shakespearean sonnets: lyric, iambic pentameter, quatrains, couplet, epigrammatic closure, rhyme scheme, origins in thirteenth-century Italy, even, I suppose, "the dark lady," but nothing of the soul, nothing of the passion for language and living and human diversity that surely must have driven Shakespeare to write.

Rebekah "dreaded" interpreting poetry, too. Not that assigning meaning is something alien to adolescents: they readily critique parents, teachers, peers, films, fashion, and food. But when assigning meaning to poems, Rebekah felt her intellect was always on the line and it always fell short. "It seemed that everyone else got some deep meaning from a poem, and I just thought it was a nice poem."

If reading and writing poetry is a test that students win or lose, many will reject it. That distresses me. I want poetry to be my students' companion.

As my wife and I prepared to move to Utah in 1991, I decided that my days lugging furniture and loading a rental truck were over. I contacted a national moving company. Kathy and I had packed and labeled more than one hundred cardboard boxes. My interest was locating books once I got to Utah, so I had boxes labeled "fiction," "poetry," "reading theory," "literacy," "cookbooks," etc.

Two weeks after workers hauled out our belongings, the massive moving van showed up at our new digs in Logan, Utah. The husband-and-wife team that orchestrated the move had picked up three helpers in Salt Lake City, an insoucient, careless crew. Dents and dings were the order of the day.

One remarkable moment stands out in my mind, though: One helper, sporting a faded concert T-shirt and wispy goatee, approached me where I worked in the garage. Sweat dripped from his chin as he clutched a heavy cardboard box to his chest.

"Sir," he said, "where's your poetry go?"

A more profoundly philosophical question I've never been asked.

My answer is simple. Poetry goes in our daily lives. It goes in our hearts and minds and bones, in the very blood that courses through our veins and sustains the life of every cell. Everywhere we go, then, poetry goes with us.

And it certainly goes in multigenre papers, just as I believe it goes in kindergarten through graduate school across every discipline.

As a language arts teacher, I am most concerned with students' development in using language. I want people to get better and better at it. Living with poetry can help that happen. Poetry is a place of precision and imagination in language. The genre requires visual thinking and exercises our capacity to synthesize, analyze, construct meaning, and feel emotion—a marvelous combination of cognition and affect. Poetry asks that we live metaphor, connect, associate, and experience epiphany. Poetry makes us focus.

Twelve years ago I started a ritual in my classes, workshops, and presentations: In the opening minutes I read aloud a poem, usually a contemporary free-verse poem. I give the poem the best reading I can, letting the words lead me to pauses, inflections, and changes in rhythm. If someone requests it, I reread the poem. Unless someone offers comment, though, we don't discuss it. And I certainly don't explain what I think the poem means. Listening is enough.

This poetry ritual takes minutes, sometimes seconds. The daily reading sets up a pleasurable, predictable routine. It also demonstrates my value for poetry, its accessibility, and the critical difference that reading aloud makes in understanding it. Listeners get to hear the voice of a modern poet they probably don't know. When I taught high school, this ritual meant ninety positive experiences with contemporary poetry every semester, regardless of what else we were studying. Every day students heard the language of poetry: crafted, focused, condensed, and, as William Stafford (1986) has written, "with a little luck in it" (97).

To consolidate the connection my students make with poetry, I not only have them read it and listen to it—I have them write it. Because of experiences with poetry like Rebekah's, this is a time of trepidation for many students. But William Stafford gives good advice about writing poems, advice that can remove the pressure:

You could tell about something that actually happens. Don't make up anything at first. Just tell it. You will not tell *everything*. That is impossible. But you tell what seems most helpful to tell, what you think about when you remember . . . . Don't try ahead of time to decide what will be important: trust your feelings, let them guide you. (Quoted in Janeczko 1983, 112)

In helping students discover topics for poems, I often lead them into "quick writes" as I've seen middle school teacher and author Linda Rief do. I give them the start of a line and ask students to follow it, writing rapidly for two minutes without self-censorship. Frequently, they uncover language and perceptions that might lead to a poem. One start I have used with sixth graders through graduate students is "When I was . . ." I ask them to pick a year of their life and let language fly. Undergraduate Allison Olsen wrote this:

When I was 19 I was already married and divorced. I—we—knew it wouldn't last but did it anyway. After a week of marriage he mentioned divorce. It finally happened a year and a half later.

After we had done three or four quick writes, I asked students to choose one that looked promising for further writing and to take a few minutes to cluster images and language the quick write brought to mind. Figure 15–1 shows what Allison jotted:

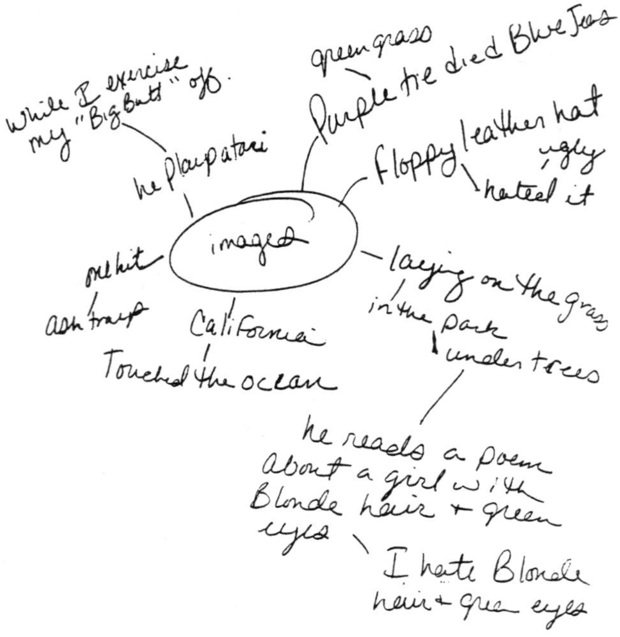

FIGURE 15–1. *Allison Olsen's handwritten clustering.*

Out of this, Allison wrote a poem that dives to the heart of impetuous young love and adults who hurt but don't help:

She Knew

You took me to California
and I touched the ocean
for the very first time.

We rode the carousel
on the boardwalk
and you asked me to be
your wife.

I said yes
and we drove
home for two days.

Your mother flew round trip
in one day
to see our wedding.
Her eyes were so swollen
from crying
that she didn't
take her sunglasses off,
                              even once.

She was crying for us,
for you.
She knew you would hurt,
and cry,
when I left you.

> Allison Olsen, Junior,
> Utah State University

In her final learning portfolio, Allison explains:

My attempts at poetry were the hardest thing I had to do all quarter. It was hard enough to get personal thoughts or feeling on paper, in ink, because of the permanence . . . . It was even harder to share those poems with other people, but I did . . . . I wrote "She Knew" the night after we practiced doing quick writes and clustering exercises . . . . I would have told anyone before that night that those prewriting gimmicks just didn't work with me. I was wrong.

The key to making a poem and not just feeling an emotion is getting down to writing. The night after Allison clustered images about her first marriage, she did just that. Mary Oliver metaphorically points out why getting down to writing is crucial:

If Romeo and Juliet had made appointments to meet, in the moon-light-swept orchard, in all the peril and sweetness of conspiracy, and then more often than not failed to meet—one or the other lagging, or afraid, or busy elsewhere—there would have been no romance, no passion, none of the drama for which we remember and celebrate them. Writing a poem is not so different—it is a kind of possible love affair between something like the heart (that courageous but also shy factory of emotion) and the learned skills of the conscious mind. They make appointments with each other, and keep them, and something begins to happen. (7)

Allison wrote the quick write, clustered images, then made an appointment. She did not lag, she was not afraid, she didn't busy herself elsewhere. She kept the appointment and something happened.

APPOINTMENTS

Throughout the process of writing multigenre papers, I arrange appointments for students to write during class time. I lead them into writing and revision, me frequently working right along with them. A "non-negotiable" of my teaching is engagement with language on paper. There is no substitute for that—not a brilliant lecture about topic choice, not peer group conferences, not the words of excellent writers, not advanced computer skills, not a surefire form for writing essays. The act of writing is all—humble and irreplaceable. Whether kindergartner or national book award winner, the writer must put words on paper, must, a student explained to me once, develop a "writing state of mind." With such a mind-set students are able to recognize topics and go without hesitation to the writing. This holds true whether the writing is supercharged or tedious, whether the writer is clipping along at top speed or slogging through one agonized phrase at a time. Regardless of how it is done, the act of writing—making appointments and keeping them—is invaluable and eminently worthy of class time.

Fourth-grade teacher Jill Heffner explains it well:

I positively loved the "free" writing in class. There were times at home when I just sat in front of the computer, knowing basically what I wanted to write about, but distracted to the point of debilitation. When I was there in your classroom, it was different. Distractions turned into ideas, and ideas turned into pieces. I was very comfortable writing *with* you and the others. There was a certain understood focus.

I want poetry to arise naturally in students' multigenre papers, and it does, especially the deeper they become immersed in their subject. But I also arrange appointments for students to take advantage of that "understood focus" of our classroom, to develop the habit and discipline of writing. Here are four poetry appointments you might try with your students.

Found Poetry

This assignment cues students to look for poems hidden within the prose of textbooks, magazines, newspapers, novels, pamphlets, memos, and letters. Occasionally, the writers of these various forms create passages of rhythm, imagery, surprise, and impact. With a little arranging on the page, these words stand as rescued poems. I ask students to find such passages and photocopy the original words so we can see their origin.

To introduce my English methods students to a contemporary, female, African American novelist and a feminist view on issues of gender, interracial marriage, slavery, literacy, and violence, especially as they played out in the antebellum South, we read Octavia Butler's *Kindred* (1979). Butler's absorbing novel—both historical and realistic, with a touch of science fiction—is perfect for study, discussion, and enjoyment in English and social studies upper-grade high school classes. I ask students to find a passage of Butler's crisp prose suitable for turning into a found poem. Here is a passage a student rescued, when the narrator, Dana, finds herself lost in strange but somehow familiar surroundings:

> I found the road and followed it, listening for the dogs. But now, only a few night birds and insects broke the silence—crickets, an owl, some other bird I had no name for. I hugged the side of the road, trying to suppress my nervousness and praying to go home.
>
> Something dashed across the road so close to me that it almost brushed my leg. I froze, too terrified even to scream, then realized that it was just some small animal that I had frightened—a fox. (34)

The student shaped this poem out of Butler's words, his decisions on lineation highlighting surprises and information:

Foxes and Dogs

I found the road
and followed it,
listening for the dogs.

but now,
only a few birds
and insects
broke the silence—

crickets,
an owl,
some other bird I had no name for.

Ihuggedthesideoftheroad,tryingtosuppressmynervousness

and praying to go home.
Something dashed across the road
so close to me that it almost brushed
      my leg.

I froze,

too terrified even to scream,

then realized that it was just some small animal
that
I
had frightened—

a fox

Byron Stepherson, Junior,
Utah State University

    Found poetry is an easy introduction to much of what we value in po-
etry: compressed language, form, skillful diction, rhythm, and clear meaning.
Students practice manipulating language on the page without having to generate it. Many students skeptical of this assignment are surprised by what
they find.

Haiku

I have rediscovered this Japanese form that was my introduction to writing
poetry twenty-seven years ago . . . with some new, liberating understandings
of it.

    As a young teacher in search of poetry "activities" for my creative writing
students, I came upon journal articles about haiku that explained its merits
and described its form. You know the form, of course: three lines, the first
line of five syllables, the second of seven, the third of five. My students
wrote haiku, and I evaluated it with a keen, quantitative eye. I awarded As,
Bs, and Cs based upon how well the writer adhered to the five-seven-five
syllabication pattern. Evaluation of writing was never simpler for me and
clearer for students

and never was it more off the mark.

    What mattered, my grading habits proclaimed, was form, not content;
syllabication, not meaning. I found myself awarding As to mediocre haiku
because the syllabication was correct and Bs and Cs to great haiku because
their syllabication was not.

    Recently, two former students—both English teachers now—bought
me *The Essential Haiku: Versions of Bashō, Buson, and Issa* (1994), edited and
translated by former poet laureate Robert Hass. It is a wonderful book, the
haiku by the Japanese masters playful, surprising, and poignant; the com-
mentary by Hass informative, scholarly, and pragmatic about haiku's origins,
evolution, and traditions:

If the first level of a haiku is its location in nature, its second is almost always some implicit Buddhist reflection on nature. One of the striking differences between Christian and Buddhist thought is that in the Christian sense of things, nature is fallen, and in the Buddhist sense it isn't. Another is that, because there is no creator-being in Buddhist cosmology, there is no higher plane of meaning to which nature refers. (xiii)

Hass barely mentions (a mere half page on 299) the prime criteria by which I exactly measured haiku success in my mid-1970s classroom—the 5-7-5 syllabication pattern. In his translations, in fact, Hass doesn't try to get the syllable count right. What he strives hard to capture, however, is the poet's perception, the swift observation, the pure image, the sometimes playful attitude of the haiku master.

Haiku "have a quality of actuality," writes Hass, "of the moment seized on and rendered purely, and because of this they seem to elude being either traditional images of nature or ideas about it" (xiv).

This notion of the "moment seized on and rendered purely" without explanation is precisely what leads many students to respond to haiku this way: "Huh?" Students aren't practiced in reading such poetry. Through most of their schooling they have read poetry that rhymes and has clear meanings. Shel Silverstein and Jack Prelutsky come to mind. Verse delightful, musical, and heavily rhymed. So definitive does this idea of poetry become in students that it is not uncommon for them in later years to resist the notion that a free-verse poem is even poetry at all.

Like haiku, contemporary free verse—what I'd like my contemporary students to write—revels in imagery and original description, in personal and implicit meaning. In addition to reading rhyming poets in elementary school, I'd like to see students get plenty of experience reading poets of image and natural speech. In secondary school and college I'd like to see curricula move away from the chronological historical study of literature, which often guarantees that students will read only poets who used strict rhyme and meter, however brilliantly.

Haiku moves us to see. And that's what we want our students to do through poetry.

Matsuo Bashō (1644–1694) writes:

> A bee
> staggers out
> of the peony. (18)

Because image and perception are most important in haiku, they are wonderful for discussing precisely what we see; students get opportunity to flex their reader response muscles. In Bashō's haiku, I'm right there in an eye-level close-up of the flower, noting the bee's unsteady departure from the peony, loving the word *staggers,* and imagining the Bacchanalian delight bees might take from sucking nectar.

Another Bashō haiku:

> The dragonfly
> can't quite land
> on that blade of grass. (45)

Writing haiku is like painting miniatures, focusing our attention, using our everyday language to sharpen sight. And if what we write is idiosyncratic or mysterious, so be it. Of haiku Bashō said,

The profit . . . lies in making common speech right. (235)

The bones of haikai are plainness and oddness. A verse that has something interesting in it is all right, even if its meaning isn't very clear. (238)

The term *haiku* evolved partly out of the word *haikai* (304), which Hass tells us, "means 'sportive or playful'" (299). Many of the haiku Hass includes have this quality: drunken bees reeling their way hiveward, dragonflies unable to find suitable landing pads. Take a look at a haiku by Kobayashi Issa (1763–1827):

> Don't worry, spiders,
> I keep house
> casually. (153)

Hass also points out that haiku poets sometimes played a kind of call-and-response game. An opening line would be uttered and the poets created a response. I saw Hass perform this call-and-response game with a small group of students on a segment of Bill Moyers' *Poetry: The Language of Life* (1995). It's fun and profitable to try this with students. Here is a call-and-response haiku from Issa:

> Even with insects—
> some can sing,
> some can't. (163)

With my new understandings in mind, I tried out haiku one summer at the University of New Hampshire. I've spent eight summers teaching at UNH since 1987. It is always good to go back to Durham, where I earned my Ph.D. and developed deep affection for so many people. I must admit, though, that another draw for me to coastal New Hampshire is the seafood.

One of the first places I stop is Newick's, a huge barn of a seafood restaurant on Great Bay, midway between Durham and Portsmouth. No reservations. No air conditioning. No pretense. Just plastic cups, paper plates, and seafood aplenty. *Sportive* and *playful* were in my mind on one of my visits. I wrote a cycle of swift observations and pure images:

Newick's Haiku

Circling fans whir
above five hundred
    fish eaters.

Setting sunlight
over the bay
    gleams on a lifted fork.

Waitresses run, sweat,
glide and hip through tables.
"We cruise," says one.

Calamari, oysters, native shrimp—
sold out
    again.

July 4th Special:
Lobster, clam chowder, Sam Adams:
    Red, white, and brew.*

Plates of clams:
stepstones up
    the waitress's arm.

T-shirted, gap-toothed child
done eating
    slaps waves of rhythm on her knees.

Dinner arrives:
a tangle
    of fried.

Eat healthy:
broiled seafood—
    not on my life.

Romano sits with journal:
Bashō in bluejeans,
    tartar sauce on his chin.

---

*This is a "found" haiku, a Newick's holiday lobster promotion I read as I stood in line.

In Tim King's communication class, a student wrote this haiku and taught me something about one kind of rose:

> Lavender rose
> Blooming in the light
> With its thornless stem
> Through the sky.

> Victoria Stone, Sophomore, Mason High School
> Mason, Ohio

Art teacher Kerry Kronenberger's multigenre paper about her trip to Paris took the form of a scrapbook containing her writing and drawing and photographs. It included this haiku:

> Oh Leonardo
> Are those dainty lips smiling
> At you or at me?

Eighth-grade language arts teacher Roni Carpenter wrote about cats, combining research, feelings, and particularities about Maris, her tortoise-shell cat named after the New York Yankee slugger:

> Sleeping with cats is
> A sensuous luxury—
> Fur and purrs and dreams.

Photograph Poem

In Chapter 7 we saw how Jeri Meyer incorporated a photo into her lead. From there Jeri's readers go on to learn about pain, deception, distance, and loss. The last photo, then, of twelve-year-old Jeri and her father dancing with gleeful abandon is a devastating and poignant conclusion to her paper. As a reader, the photo is all I needed.

Students may, however, use a photograph as a creative springboard to dive deeply with language into a topic. Coupled with photo, words can take readers—and the writer—further in understanding. The writer might describe a photo, or interpret it, or describe pertinent information that isn't apparent by the picture alone. The very act of using language to describe the image often leads the writer to surprising perceptions and understanding.

College junior Stephanie Musselman (see Chapter 9) wrote a painful, sympathetic, and loving multigenre paper about her father, including the divorce of her parents and eventual breakup of the family. Inspired by a snapshot of her mother and father as teenagers on prom night, Stephanie composed this poem in second person, addressed to her mother. Stephanie describes, provides information the photo cannot reveal, and interprets:

Photograph, 1962

The dress is second hand,
Robins egg blue with
Velvet gloves to match.
He's proud, red face beaming,
hand clenched tightly at his side.
You look aside, shyly, as he
Faces the camera,
smiling at your mother; this is
the eleventh photograph she's taken.
Her baby, her first born, her Connie,
is in love
with the man whom she will spend
twenty-two tumultuous years.

Later you all drive to Rose Hill Cemetery
to show your cool confidence of mysteries
unexplained; a statue in the night who moves
Dreamily through the cemetery,
Unaware of her destined resting place.
You are young and your dreams pervade the
Nightmares you cannot anticipate.
The sound of "Just A Dream" lingers through
his Chevy, through the moist spring air.
It plays in his car, at the prom,
and in your head that night and for
Many years to come.

It is a dream, you two together.

- Ask students to bring to class three or four photos of their subject matter.
- Put students in small groups. (Three makes an intimate group with plenty of time to share.) Their job is to talk about the photos, explaining context, asking questions, telling background stories, describing future events of the characters. The important thing is to get a lot of language flowing about the photos.
- Move students out of groups and into appointments with one of the photos. Provide ten or fifteen minutes for focused writing.
- In the days ahead shape the writing into poems (or some other genre if the writing wants to go that way).

Prose Poem

Donna Bernhisel used a photograph from the 1930s to spark writing that took her further into the experience of her grandmother, who had suffered poverty in dust bowl Oklahoma, the needless death of a child, and a long marriage to a callous husband. When I met Donna at Utah State University, she was an accomplished writer already. For her master's degree she wrote a cohesive collection of poetry that seemed ready for publication. In Donna's multigenre paper she included a prose poem that took its inspiration from a photograph. It isn't often that I see prose poems in students' work; it wasn't a form I made appointments for students to write. I'm still learning about it myself. Mary Oliver (1994) says this about the prose poem:

> What you see on the page is a fairly short block of type—a paragraph or two, rarely more than a page. It looks like prose. Perhaps it has characters, perhaps not. Often, it is pure description. It usually does have the same sense of difference from worldly or sequential time that one feels in a poem. And it does certainly ask to be read with the same concentration, and allowance for the fanciful and the experimental, that we give to the poem.
>
> Because the prose poem is brief . . . it seems more often than not to have at its center a situation rather than a narrative. Nothing much *happens,* that is, except this: through particularly fresh and intense writing, something happens to the reader—one's felt response to the "situation" of the prose poem grows fresh and intense also.
>
> What is especially fascinating about prose poems is the problem of making the language work without the *musicality of the line.* The syntax found in prose poems is often particularly exquisite, combining power and grace. (86–87)

In third person Donna explores her grandmother's thoughts and feelings as a young mother in a situation she imagines out of the photo:

August 11, 1936

She remembers on the day the picture was taken that she worried most about leaking. Breast milk soaking through the worn cotton print, her breasts swinging hard as potatoes against her when the truck bumped over holes in the highway. She remembers exactly the smell of her sweat mixing with her baby's hair, cradled in her arms, trying to let her sleep in the rocking truck. Wind whistled through the tarp stretched tight above the bed of the truck where she sat. It was hard to nurse her baby in the truck with two men she hardly knew. She wasn't like those backwoods women who nursed on a street corner like some dairy cow. She remembers most the ache of wanting to feed her baby. Baby's sweating hair pressing against her cotton dress. Having to wait. Wanting silence, no wind. Just quiet, her baby pressing hard against her. Rubbing its mouth against the cloth of her dress. Then the sharp pain of release and milk spreading warm down her front. The baby rubbing against her, quieted by the smell, the taste of her. Wind whistling between them.

Donna Bernhisel, Graduate Student,
Utah State University

Fresh, intense, powerful, and graceful, just as Oliver said. And, I would add, senseful.

Poems for Two Voices

More often than I'd like to admit, the elitist undergraduate English major marches forth in me. When I first heard elementary school teacher friends praise Paul Fleischman's *Joyful Noise: Poems for Two Voices* (1988), I was skeptical. Two voices? What kind of gimmick was this? I'd been to poetry readings by renowned poets like Rita Dove, William Stafford, Mark Strand, Seamus Heaney, and MeKeel McBride. I'd never heard them read a poem for two voices.

I kept my disdain to myself, though, since so many of my friends liked these poems. My insufferable condescension ended abruptly one evening when a student asked if I would help her read a poem for two voices she had written. Reading this kind of poem aloud is a key to appreciating it. The two voices bring life to language, words crafted and dramatic, sometimes separate, sometimes together when words appear on the same line.

The poem Mary asked me to read was part of her multigenre paper about the Jewish Holocaust during the 1930s and 1940s. Although Mary had read *The Diary of Anne Frank*, she'd never really investigated the Jewish Holocaust. She did for this paper. Mary read several books and watched *Night and Fog* (1955) and *Schindler's List* (1993). The most important part of her research, however, was the interview she conducted with a concentration camp survivor, Katherine Millard, her fiancé's gypsy mother. Mary also took notes as she watched a videotaped interview with another survivor, Pearl Levy, the mother of one of Mary's colleagues.

Mary took the stories the two survivors told and the language with which they told them and shaped this poem for two voices:

PEARL LEVY	KATHERINE MILLARD
In the night	
All Jews report to the school	In the night
	Gypsies were taken
We carried a five pound package	
	We had nothing but our clothes
We stayed four days	
Then we moved to a ghetto	
In the middle of the night	In the middle of the night
my mom	my mom
father	father
sister and her four children	
	my five brothers
three	
	four
sisters	sisters
In cattle cars	In cattle cars
no daylight	no daylight
Ten days to get there	
Throw out the dead and waste	
Auschwitz	Auschwitz
horrible camp	

not good place

Who shall live?

Who shall die?
Dr. Joseph Mangele
Angel of Death

My mother
father
sister and her four children

All to the left
my
sisters

I never saw them again
my two
sisters
and myself to the right

We kept only our shoes
Shaved
Disinfected

Thirty people on boards

No blankets
Skeletons starved
mostly bread and water
Potatoes

Barbed wire
Some go everyday
to die

In the morning
picked up

Thousands burned
Smell horrible

more people burned
more potatoes we'd have

my job
pick out clothes for the dead
Dig
Dig ditches

My mother
father

my five brothers

my three
sisters

I never saw them again
my
sister

We kept our clothes

Shaved
Disinfected
Tattooed

People crowded on the floor
No blankets
Skeletons starved
mostly bread and water
Potatoes

Barbed wire

to die

In the morning

bodies piled up
Thousands burned

only see the fire, no smoke

my job

Dig potatoes

What happened once

When I saw

One baby killed

head banged against the wall

No sorrow
We didn't cry

        Twenty of us girls

        put in the gas chamber

        SS took us out
        No sorrow
        We didn't cry

Mary Millard, Clear View Alternative Intermediate School,
League City, Texas

That night in class as I knelt beside Mary and read the poem with her, our voices, the subject matter, and Mary's craft transfixing class members seated around the seminar table, I'd never concentrated harder on reading well. Mary's poem means a great deal to me. I wanted to print it here not only for its merit as a poem for two voices, but also because it is a poem that ought to be circulated among teachers who care about humanity and teach about holocausts, who want to reaffirm the message "Never Again." Since that night, I have made sure to introduce my classes to the possibility of writing a poem for two voices. Recently one of my students wrote a multigenre paper about rape on Miami's campus. In the following poem, Jenn creates the voices of the man and woman involved. Not uncommon in cases of rape, they knew each other.

The Last Word

He said

You were drunk.

You passed out,
   you slut.
   I knew what you wanted;
   I know everything about you,
   don't I?
I knew you once

I can't stand you.
You're ruining my life
   making such a huge deal of
One stupid night

She said

You were drunk.
   I was drunk.
   I drank so much
I passed out.

I knew you once—
   I never thought you'd do this.
   I don't know who you are now.

I can't stand you.
You're ruining my life.

One stupid night—
   one I'll never forget,
   thanks to you.
   I don't know who to blame
   for any of this.
   You haunt me

Whenever I see you on campus,
    You squirm inside, don't you?
    Why are you so uncomfortable?
    Why are you crying?
No matter how hard I try,
I'll never understand

Whenever I see you on campus.

No matter how hard I try,
I'll never understand
    why you felt you had the right
    to do what you did.
    And now you have
All the control.

All the control
    is mine now, isn't it?
    I didn't just invade your body,
I invaded your life.

—My life
    will never be the same.
    It's not fair—
    you can sleep with the lights
        off;

I can't
    believe this;
    you're overreacting!
    I never meant to hurt you.

I can't.

I didn't do anything wrong!
You never said no!

I didn't do anything wrong!

I never said yes.

Jenn Reid, Junior,
Miami University

Jenn's and Mary's poems are grim and sobering. They illuminate the dark side of human experience, but those experiences are real and the truths surrounding them need to be told. The poems make me thoughtful, sympathetic, knowledgeable, and respectful, determined to teach about holocausts and violence to women.

But I like to smile and laugh upon this earth, too, so I'll end this section with a light poem for two voices. Sara Boose wrote about her life as the one female—third oldest—among five brothers. There is humor throughout Sara's multigenre paper, "My Brothers and Me," but also plenty of childhood and adolescent pain that arose from gender differences, puberty, and immaturity. Sara became so passionate about her project that she spent hours learning HyperStudio techniques and translating the paper to a multimedia format. Here is her poem for two voices that captures the perspectives of Sara, then six, and her father at the birth of the last child:

DAD

It's a boy!
How exciting!

ME

It's a boy?

	Oh, no.
That makes five!	That makes five.
We named him Matthew James.	
	Please tell me it's not *another* boy.
Do	What am I going to
you want to go to the hospital	do?
to see him?	
	The last thing I want to do is see
	him.
All that hoping and praying	All that hoping and praying
paid off.	
	was for
Nothing	nothing.
went wrong—your mother and	
Matthew are fine.	
	I even asked god to send me a
	sister.
	I said,
Dear God	"Dear God . . ."
thank you for blessing our family	
with another healthy baby.	
I can't believe it!	I can't believe it.
It's a boy!	It's a boy.

- Share aloud a number of poems for two voices so that students get a rhythmical sense of them. Point out how the voices speak both separately and together.
- Ask students to take two characters from their material whose perspectives are similar (as Katherine Millard's and Pearl Levy's are) or different (as Sara's and her father's are) or diametrically opposed (as He and She are in "The Last Word").
- Instruct students to play with words the characters might say. Let the characters speak their truths and experience about a particular topic, sometimes converging in exact words they can say together.
- Shape the poem over a period of days.

NOT ONE STUDENT

Mary Millard uses Jewish Holocaust survivors' words to take us inside women who testify about a time when evil was most free. Jenn Reid reveals psychological burdens and blind rationalizations that follow rape. Sara Boose reveals vastly different perspectives at the birth of a baby. All three women confidently used a particular poetic form to communicate hard-won truth.

Our students must read poetry that gives them faith that they, too, might successfully try the genre. Reading Marge Piercy's poetry did that for me in the 1970s. Ten weeks of literary study of Shakespeare's sonnets did not do that for Rebekah. It did the opposite, in fact. She saw no room in the world of poetry for her own voice and perception, so unready developmentally was she in tenth grade for an intense and, perhaps, pedantic study of the minutia and formal features of a poetic subgenre that has a long history in the Western literary canon.

In closing, I'll stand by this: All the writing in anybody's idea of a literary canon is not worth turning away one student from reading or writing a poem.

BOOKS TO HELP MAKE APPOINTMENTS
TO WRITE POETRY

BEHN, ROBIN, and CHASE TWITCHELL, eds. 1992. *The Practice of Poetry: Writing Exercises from Poets Who Teach*. New York: HarperCollins.

GROSSMAN, FLORENCE. 1982. *Getting From Here To There: Writing and Reading Poetry*. Montclair, NJ: Boynton/Cook.

HEARD, GEORGIA. 1995. *Writing Toward Home: Tales and Lessons to Find Your Way*. Portsmouth, NH: Heinemann.

————. 1989. *For the Good of the Earth and Sun: Teaching Poetry*. Portsmouth, NH: Heinemann.

JOHNSON, DAVID. 1990. *Word Weaving*. Urbana, IL: NCTE.

MICHAELS, JUDITH ROWE. 1999. *Risking Intensity: Reading and Writing Poetry with High School Students*. Urbana, IL: NCTE.

STAFFORD, WILLIAM, and STEPHEN DUNNING. 1992. *Getting the Knack: 20 Poetry Writing Exercises*. Urbana, IL: NCTE

TSUJIMOTO, JOE. 1988. *Teaching Poetry Writing to Adolescents*. Urbana, IL: NCTE.

16 | TEACHER EXPERTISE
Branching Off

High school teacher Nanci Bush tells me how her students began "branching off" from the idea of the multigenre project as only writing. Although this book is about helping students and teachers write effective and coherent written texts, many teachers have talked to me about the "branching off" their students have done. Their descriptions have been thrilling.

Nanci Bush reports that one of her Solon, Ohio, students, Karen Ostberg,

[is] a pianist and composer. She chose Jim Brinkman, a local pianist [as her subject] and assembled her paper as a program that one would receive if they attended one of his concerts. Then, she composed music that was influenced by Jim Brinkman's style. She treated our class to a concert in the auditorium. She first played Brinkman's music, and then her own pieces. Another class heard what we were doing and joined us. Karen was VERY nervous about performing this type of music because she was afraid that her classmates would not enjoy or appreciate it. After several standing ovations and encores, her fears were assuaged.

Another student of Nanci's, Bridget Andrews, enjoys dance. "She chose Marilyn Monroe for her project. In addition to her written composition, she choreographed a series of three dances depicting the rise and fall of Marilyn." These dances she performed and videotaped.

Becky Hoag, a high school teacher in San Antonio, Texas, exuberantly describes Joy Jauer's oral presentation about Monet:

[Joy] dressed in a suit, put her hair in a bun, wore high heels and became a Parisian gallery curator. She brought in easels where she displayed Monet prints and walked us through his stages of development as an artist. Wait! That's not all! She brought in a partially painted reproduction of his water lilies and paint and illustrated the technique in class.

Sirpa Grierson of BYU writes about the variety of formats that multi-genre projects have taken:

> Even the form that the writings come in has taken on a life of its own: photograph albums, journals, scrolls, Nerd's candy containers (Roald Dahl, of course), and canning jars have appeared as I have asked students to tie their final product together in some manner. Responses often take on the time period or personality of the subject. A red beach ball plastered with crots hangs in my office for Ray Bradbury's *Martian Chronicles,* on my shelf is a sheaf of hand-made papers in an antique container for Hermann Hesse's *Siddhartha,* and a quilt on 1800s reproduction fabric representing Jo in Louisa May Alcott's *Little Women.* The variety has been endless.

My own students have written memorable multigenre papers, though they haven't branched off in such multiple intellectual ways that my friends and colleagues report. Nevertheless, the final class meeting(s) when they present their papers is informative, entertaining, and often moving. In a recent class one student after another drew us into their particular multigenre world. Papers about sexual assault on Miami's campus; a beloved grandparent; the pace and compromises involved in raising a child, tending bar, and attending school full-time; the attachment a student developed to an Appalachian family through her church's outreach humanitarian work; a relationship among three generations of mothers and daughters—the grandmother having recently died of breast cancer . . . Time slipped by that evening. We went beyond the designated end of class. I apologized for the time miscalculation but said I would stay until everyone presented. One student had to leave in order to relieve a baby-sitter. The rest stayed another forty-five minutes.

"Bottom line," wrote Sara in evaluating the evening, "I would have stayed until midnight."

17 | RISK AND EXODUS

Melinda Hill was a sophomore in college when she wrote the following multigenre paper in my creative writing class. During the first four weeks, Melinda seemed stuck, each week bringing to conference the same story with only slight alterations of its surface features. I was bent on supporting students and wishing them Godspeed in their writing, but I was losing patience with Melinda.

The fourth conference I told her she just seemed to be fiddling around with the scene, not really risking anything and diving deeply into the writing. I didn't feel, I said, that she was giving her all to the writing. Melinda's eyes filled with tears. She confessed that she wasn't giving the weekly writing all she could, that she had been busy with other courses, that she wasn't sure what I wanted.

I spoke some about risk and breaking loose and writing about subjects that really mattered to us. I didn't feel good after the conference. Thought I'd acted like a pedagogical bully. I could have been more tactful. Still, I had this nagging teacher-feeling that Melinda was capable of so much more than the writing she was bringing to conference each week.

That night at home my telephone rang. It was Melinda.

"Tell me what you meant about risk again?"

I never tried harder to explain myself and at the same time communicate the confidence I had in a student's talent, promise, and vision. We talked a few more minutes. I don't know about Melinda, but I sure felt better after the conversation. "I'm glad you called," I said before hanging up.

I wasn't sorry for the uncomfortable conference earlier that day. It was at least one week overdue. And it had spurred both of us to dig a little deeper, be a little better. Melinda had taken a risk in calling the teacher at home that evening and asking her important question. It made me recognize her individuality, determination, and commitment. Her call nudged me to become a better teacher.

MIRIAM'S SONG

Dear Reader,

Hello, and welcome to my life, or a little piece of it anyway. The following multigenre paper describes the seven years my mom, Sarah, was married to my stepfather, Eugene. It also involves my brother, Nathan, and I. I've woven the story of Miriam into the story of the ending of my mom and step-dad's marriage. Miriam is an Old Testament Biblical character. She was the sister of Moses and Aaron. My paper follows the exodus of the Israelites from Egypt through Miriam's eyes. She makes the journey from slavery, bitterness, and oppression to freedom and joy. I found her story a good metaphor for my own.

I have been writing about this subject matter all semester. It has been good to take a look at this painful time, and has allowed healing to begin. Healing has brought about joy in my life, and I'm learning to sing. I'm learning to sing Miriam's song.

Yours,

Melinda

Eugene

Mom married
him
when I was ten.
For seven years
he took away my
life
one angry glare
at a time
as I became a fat
shell
numbed by mounds
of cookies
sugar fixes
sweet and slippery
I hid behind
who-I-should-have-been
A good student
happy

Christian
perfect
memorable
a shallow inside
buried
under layers of
fat and
hate.

How It Began

MOM:

I need
someone
to
love
hold
stroke
care
touch
warm
caress
approve
lift
carry
lead

EUGENE:

I need
someone
to
cook
clean
yield
listen
obey
work
nurse
bang
nurture
cry
quiet

Baked Stepfather

10 cups anger
8 cups religious hypocrisy
8 cups rage
6 cups bitterness
5 cups fear
5 cups insecurity
Scant teaspoon love

Mix anger, bitterness, rage, and religious hypocrisy well. Spread over fear, covering it completely. Let love sit until cold, then sprinkle haphazardly onto the pan. Stir in insecurity. Bake at 500 degrees until hard shell has formed.

I EPHESIANS 5:22
Wives, submit to your husbands, as is fitting in the Lord.

Rule 1: Wives should be a doormat to their husbands, bowing to their every whim. They should never question, never think, never react in confusion or anger, only in quietness and modesty as is fitting a Christian woman.

DEUTERONOMY 22:5
A woman must not wear men's clothing, nor a man wear women's clothing, for the Lord your God detests anyone who does this.

Rule 2: Pants are traditionally worn by men and are therefore classified as men's clothing. Since women are not to wear men's clothing, this means women cannot wear pants and so must always wear skirts. God will get very angry at any woman who wears pants for any reason, no matter how silly a woman may look wearing a skirt in subzero temperatures.

I CORINTHIANS 11:14-15
Does not the very nature of things teach you that if a man has long hair, it is a disgrace to him, but that if a woman has long hair it is her glory? For long hair is given to her as a covering.

Rule 3: This passage quite obviously shows that women are not to cut their hair. Ever. Why cut off your glory? Split ends are not an excuse. Women's hair must not be touched by scissors.

LEVITICUS 18:22
Do not lie with a man as one lies with a woman, that is detestable.

Rule 4: Homosexuals are detestable. In no way get near them. Run from them as fast as possible. They should be avoided at all costs. Someone else can save them. It isn't our job. Avoid all things that even serve as reminders of homosexuality.

This is by no means an exhaustive list of the rules and standards of the United Church of Pentecostals. For further information, please seek out a church near you, unless they find you first.

Mom

Balance.
Eugene. Melinda. Nathan.
Push. Pull.

Work. Church. God?

Run, run.
Sleep. Sleep.
Sex. Now? No choice.

No choices.
Lost.

Submit, submit.
Subdue: Anger Passion Fun.

Lost, losing.
Cry, cry, cry.
No.

Excerpt from Miriam's Diary

My brother Moses has finally come home. He says we are going to be freed soon. That God has decided to deliver us. What God? The one who has forgotten his people. The one who has let them be oppressed for so long by the Egyptians. This God has decided to deliver us?

I have been waiting hand and foot on Pharaoh's daughter for years, and I will continue to do so for years to come. I have been beaten. I have been molested.

Freedom. I'm not sure I know what that word means.

Moses must be talking to a God that I don't know.

Mine has forgotten I exist.

Dear God.

I don't:

drink
smoke
swear (usually)
wear pants
cut my hair
listen to bad music
watch bad movies

but

I'll never
be good enough
will I?

Love,

Melinda (Age 10)

Conversation Piece

EUGENE _____	MY VOICE	MY MIND
Clean up your room	Okay	It's not messy
Sit up straight	Yes, Eugene	I am
Don't talk back	Silence	Up yours
You will never	I know	I'm more than
be anything		you'll ever be
You'll be a lousy mother	mmhmmm	You disgust me
No wonder no boys		I am what you
like you	(sniff)	made me
Pig	(chew)	Asshole
I'm only saying this		
because I love you	I know	Bullshit

Eating Disorder Blues

Gotta find me a pizza
maybe a cookie too
Hell, how 'bout the whole bag
I ain't got nothin' to lose

I've got an
eating disorder
I've got the binge
and binge and binge and binge
can't purge blues

Oh my tummy hurts
I wish I could stop
I'd really like to vomit
But each time I try I flop

I've got an
eating disorder
I've got the binge
and binge and binge and binge
can't purge blues

There ain't no boys that like me
my step-dad hates me too
I'd better try to quit eating
Or I'll be size 62

I've got an
eating disorder
I've got the binge
and binge and binge and binge
can't purge blues

Excerpt from Miriam's Diary

The God of our people has shown his hand. He has killed the first born of all the Egyptians. They all died last night, quietly, while they were asleep. All their mothers went in this morning to wake them and . . .

Pharaoh will now let us go. Go? Into the desert. Into starvation and uncertainty. It almost seems better to stay. At least we have food in our mouths and a roof over our heads, even if we are slaves.

We leave in the morning.

Spock looks down at his tricorder. The planet around them is wooded, with wind rustling the trees.

Spock: I'm picking up something strange, Captain.

Kirk puts his hands on his hips.

Kirk: What . . . could it . . . be?

Spock: I'm not at all certain. It looks to be about five feet nine inches tall, wearing boots, a flannel shirt, and a pair of blue jeans. It seems angry and very unreasonable.

Kirk [looking a bit nervous]: Set your phasers . . . on . . . kill.

Suddenly the creature jumps out of the woods.

Scotty: Good God, Captain, I've never seen something so horrible.

Kirk: What are you?

Creature: I'm Eugene.

Scotty: We've heard all about you. It's known all over the galaxy, how you treat Melinda and Nathan . . .

"Nathan!" Eugene barks.

"What?"

"Get up here and clean up this mess. I tell you I've never seen such a lazy, no-good . . ."

Dear Nathan,

I'm sorry.
I wanted to protect you.
I wanted to step in and make the monster go away.

I wanted to fight for you and keep you warm and make
all the fear and cold and pain and anger go away.

I wanted to cradle you and lullaby you to sleep.

But

I couldn't even

save myself.

Love,

Your sister

Excerpt from Miriam's Diary

The route Moses is leading us on will end at the Red Sea. There is no way we can get across. We are trapped. I can see a faint cloud rising behind us.

A cloud raised by horses hooves and chariot wheels.

Pharaoh is coming after us. Either he will take us back into slavery or drive us into the sea.

God has led us out here to die. We have displeased him. We have tried, tried, tried so hard.

I can hear the sea.

Excerpt from the transcript of an interview with Eugene that appeared in the article "Sticks and Stones: The Dynamics of Verbal Abuse" in Aug. 1993 issue of *Psychology Today*.

Reporter: Do you believe you are a loving man?

Eugene: Now what exactly is love anyway? I'll tell you what it is. Love is authority. Rules and following them. God is strict. He expects perfection of us and I expect perfection out of the kids.

Reporter: Isn't that a bit unreasonable?

Eugene: Unreasonable?! That's always been what's expected out of me. Why, I remember when I was a boy, I had to get up early, do all my chores, and be scrubbed and ready for breakfast by 6 a.m. Everything had to be done right, too, or I'd get a whippin' like you wouldn't believe.

Reporter: So your father abused you . . .

Eugene: That warn't no abuse. He loved me. He kept me in line. That's what family is. That's what family does. That's love.

Reporter: Have you ever whipped your step-children, Melinda and Nathan?

Eugene: No. Not yet. If they keep pushing though . . .

Reporter: What do you think of Melinda and Nathan?

Eugene: Lazy as all get out. If I didn't keep at them every second of the day, nothin' would ever get done. They'd be on the road to hell if it weren't for me.

Reporter: Hell?

Eugene: I taught them the rules, what they had to do to be right in God's sight. And I make sure they stick with 'em. If it weren't for me, I don't know where they'd be.

Excerpt from Miriam's Diary

I am on the other side of the Red Sea.

God has seen us! He has freed us. Moses raised his staff and the Red Sea parted, like curtains pulled by invisible hands. Then a cloud fell between us and the Egyptians, and all night we crossed the sea bed.

As the last family set foot on the other side, Pharaoh entered the dry sea bed with his troops. Soon they were all in the middle of the two walls of water. They were so close. We hadn't moved, couldn't. Moses stood calmly, then, he lowered his staff, and the curtains of water fell.

I watched them drown. Our captors, our rapists. I heard them scream. I watched their bodies float to the surface.

We were free.

God had remembered us.

God had freed us.

After a few moments of stunned silence, Moses began to sing. One by one, others joined in.

I will sing to the Lord
for he is highly exalted
The horse and its rider
he has hurled into the sea

The Lord is my strength
I will praise him
Pharaoh's chariots and his army
he has hurled into the sea
The deep waters have covered them

In your unfailing love
You will lead
The people you have
redeemed

I began to cry. I picked up a dusty tambourine, long silent, and began to dance and sing. I danced up and down the shore, and other women began to follow, leaping and singing. We kicked and spun and cried and sang

I will sing to the Lord
for he is highly exalted
The horse and its rider
he has hurled into the sea

He has redeemed us. We are free.

Dear Eugene,

I know you are wondering why I am leaving. The better question is, why did I marry an asshole like you in the first place. I have a few ideas.

I needed to be loved. I needed to be held. I wanted to be wanted. My first husband was gay. I needed someone to be attracted to me as a woman. You were.

And then . . . it was easier to stay. The Bible says divorce is wrong, so I thought I should stick it out. It's better for the kids that way.

I lost myself somewhere. I'm not sure where I was those seven years. Seven years of cowering, fearing. Then one day . . . I said no.

And that was the end of that.

It sounds easier than it is. Codependency is hard to explain unless you are there. I love you. I do.

But you only love yourself, your rules. You cling to them and your God-given authority. I hope you find a wonderful new woman to screw soon.

Good-bye

Love

Sarah

Psalm

Then we cut our hair and
Danced a freedom song
on the banks of the Red Sea
Tambourines singing
Praising
He-who-hasn't-forgotten

Never look back
run from the flood
tease the wind
dance on the shore

Unafraid of the storms
Blinded by the sudden light
The horse and rider
thrown

Surely goodness and mercy
will follow us

Amen

End Notes

The content of Miriam's diary was taken and expanded from Exodus 12–15 in the Old Testament of the Bible. Miriam's thoughts and emotions were added by me. The song she sings and her dancing are taken from the Bible.

The play Nathan imagines was loosely based on the *Star Trek* franchise.

18 | INDELIBLE MOMENTS, CENTRAL ACTS, CRUCIAL THINGS, MEANINGFUL PLACES

INDELIBLE MOMENTS

I have written before about bright moments, a term I borrowed from jazz saxophonist and composer Rahsaan Roland Kirk (1973). Bright moments are indelible. They are happiness, joy, and ecstasy. Life without them would be bleak. My life, for example, would be less without these bright moments:

. . . my daughter at her first swim meet—she seven—holding her position after the starting gun's snap, and after every other swimmer had left the blocks and she was certain she would not false start, diving into the water and swimming that gallant first race.

. . . my father in the 1950s behind the bar in his tavern on a slow afternoon. I walk up to him, me about six. He reaches under his white apron and pulls out a palm overflowing with coins.

. . . Cathy, an undergraduate, reads to me during conference her essay about her personal relationship to Chris Crutcher's *Ironman* (1995). During our exploratory talk, she says something she realizes for the first time about the relationship between her father and her youngest brother.

. . . a fresh basil leaf from my garden, crushed between my fingers, time stopped for one breath, nothing else mattering at that moment, the fragrance saying, "Wait 'til you taste the sauce!"

Bright, indelible moments exist in our multigenre topics, too. When we render them, we show what our subject values, we show what lasts, what has positive meaning that buoys those characters through life. Laura Roth wrote a multigenre paper about her grandmother that merges family stories with information she has learned from interviews with relatives. One section of her paper is titled "Marriage and Motherhood." She began it by imagining herself into another voice and re-creating this bright moment during a time of global war, Jim Crow laws, and swinging popular music:

Streetcar Ride
August 28, 1943

From the back of the streetcar
   A Negro band headed for a party
   Practicing the latest from Ellington;
   A horn, a guitar, and a drum
They seem to be playing just for us.

Of course, they have no way of knowing
   Al in his sport coat
   Me in a baby blue dress
   Full skirt, matching shoes
How happy we are

That the minister in Newport,
   Kentucky, just across the river
   In the parlor of his home
   Believed us when we smiled and said
Yes, we're both twenty-one.

Now, new ring on my finger
   New husband at my side
   We tap our feet
   And he pecks my cheek
As the Negro band plays on.

Laura Roth, Junior,
Miami University

Indelible moments, of course, are not always bright. Sometimes they are dark and mark us forever. One of my students had long been an admirer of John Kennedy, had read books and numerous articles about him. She wrote a multigenre paper about the last few years of his life. That paper, she knew, would not be complete if she avoided the moment of his assassination. From the point of view of the dying President she imagined a stream of consciousness—a boundryless instant in time that draws in important people and moments in his life:

dear god jackie I can't see blackness oh god i've been hit blood jackie so much blood caroline . . . john . . . lets go sailing on the cape all of us together help me jackie pounding pounding why is my blood so loud jackie? oh god don't let them get her too I john fitzgerald kennedy do solemnly swear tired i'm very tired my blood is warm comforting I john take thee jacqueline can't let you go jackie I love you dear god take care of her for me . . .

Lori Livingston, Junior,
Miami University

Many characters are identified with some act or process they do so routinely that it's part of them. I couldn't imagine writing a multigenre paper about Don Murray, for example, without showing him in some way engaged in the act of writing. Mother Theresa I would have to depict interacting with the poor. My mother I would have to show mixing oil paints on a palate, or sitting in front of an easel, or framing a picture—so important was painting to her for twenty years.

Samuel Nielson wrote a multigenre paper about his grandfather, a photographer in a small Utah town. In an effective use of present tense Samuel writes about the process his grandfather was passionate about, the process he invested hours of his life in:

Give students a few minutes to think about their topics and create a quick list of indelible moments, both bright and dark, those moments that characters carry forever. Require students to be specific, to identify actual *moments,* not long stretches of time. Not "my trip to Germany after graduation," but "on the bus leaving Heidelberg when my moody traveling companion slept beside me while I stewed and stared out the window at the Black Forest." Take ten minutes or so of class time to draft an indelible moment.

Developing Film 1940s

The only place dark enough is the basement furnace room at night. Even then curtains have to be drawn to keep out moonlight. The chemicals—developer, negative intensifier, fixer, and water baths get too hot next to the furnace.

After looking about for any stray light, he takes the film by either end, like a limp u-shaped noodle, and immerses it in the developer. A daughter, allowed to be up this late to learn, sticks her head behind the curtain to keep time on her watch by moonlight. Normally, the film needs 14 minutes to develop, but since the chemicals are hotter, it will require, perhaps, only 6 minutes. He pulls the film out, fixes it in acetic acid, and washes it in clean water.

While the film dries he prepares paper for printing. He shows the daughter how to cut the light-sensitive paper into pieces with a small paper cutter. They cut 8 × 10's in fourths to reduce the need to buy more paper so soon. They make the exposures on a glass-topped box with a light inside. A hand toggle switch controls the exposure, the daughter counting the seconds out loud.

Then they huddle over the chemicals. As the first image magically materializes in the red safelight, he says, "That's Charles Olsen on leave. He was killed last week by a sniper on Okinawa. His parents will like the print and negative." A slight gurgle comes from the hand-agitated trays.

The next print shows a barefoot Tommy Jones and his dog wading out near the levee. That boy and dog were inseparable. Another print reveals Don Chadwick in his soldier browns and cap, holding a largemouth bass caught at Gunnison Reservoir. Another shows a congregation of Indian paintbrush at the foot of a grand old juniper, taken by moonlight.

He notices that his daughter is nodding off in her chair. He takes her up to her bed, making sure she's settled, and then returns.

Samuel Nielson, Graduate Student,
Utah State University

A teacher wrote about a central act of a different sort in a multigenre paper about her sexual maturation.

My Kisses

Number One
was wet and loud
as my windbreaker
gathered the impact
of his adolescent hands.
I waited
until Number 11
to feel passion
in my stomach,
not in my heart.
Numbers 12 through 18
were proof
that I could survive
the break up.
My first love
came packaged
as Number 23.
We were frustrated
and timid teens
whose lips swelled
after hours of contact.
Freshman year
in college,
I enrolled in
Kissing 101
with Numbers 30 through 42.
Numbers 43 through 66
became research subjects

for a major
in interpersonal communication.
My long term
case study,
Number 67,
interpreted experience
as love.
While he shattered
the window
with his fist,
I celebrated graduation
with Number 70.
When I said,
"Shut up and kiss me,"
Number 75 agreed.
Years later,
he wanted to love
honor and cherish
me,
while he kissed
others.
In recovery,
Number 85 said,
"I could kiss you
forever."
I rolled my eyes
and kept
kissing.

Brittany Ballard, Teacher, Mount Notre Dame High School,
Cincinnati, Ohio

THINGS CRUCIAL

Inanimate objects, concepts, ideas—things all—can hold crucial places in our lives. It is hard to imagine General Douglas
MacArthur without a long-stemmed pipe clamped between his
teeth, or tennis stars Serena and Venus Williams sans braided
hair, writer Marge Piercy without a strong feminist perspective,
my great-nephew getting about without his leg braces.

Things become identified with who we are, what we value.
We recall people from our past complete with that crucial thing
that was so characteristic of them. I flashback forty years and see
Jimmy DeMann, an old Italian immigrant I knew as a boy, slight
of height, fedora battered and sweat-stained, mustache bushy
and gray. I never saw him walking on the sidewalk in town or

My Aunt Filomina baked bread
and rolls every Friday evening for
thirty years. She kept her lawn
cut and trimmed and edged so
meticulously that my cousin said
she could be grounds keeper for
the Cleveland Indians. And in her
second kitchen in the basement
she canned hundreds of quarts of
tomato sauce every summer,
sticking a bay leaf into each jar
before screwing on the lid. These
acts and processes were central to
Aunt Filomina's life. Have students identify the central activities and processes that were part
of their characters' lives, then
draft descriptions of them.

on the side of the road beyond the village limits when he wasn't pushing his wheelbarrow.

One of my students was a passionate oarsman. In his multigenre paper about rowing, Mike wrote a poem about the shell in all its sleekness and beauty, but he wrote about it in an uncharacteristic setting, not when it was speeding across Acton Lake, but when it was at rest.

Autumn Boathouse

Feel the sharp, slick keel of the resting shell.
The wind blows in the boathouse door,
Outside red leaves flutter in crisp cool breezes.
Against your cheek, the shell is warmed cool—
The sun has been where water runs over it.
Cold hard kinetic feel
    of white shell and carbon peel.
Know the boat has gone
    where you will never go.
Know those worn shoes fit better than new,
The boat just waits for the moment.

> Mike McKernan, Junior,
> Miami University

Another student researched how she might use folktales when she began teaching. She read a lot of them and discovered their features and patterns. Here is her poem about a crucial numerical concept of the folktale:

3 and 7

There is magic here you know
The numbers tell you it will come
When it starts and when it's done

There's 3 trials or tasks and always 3 wishes
Seven dwarves and seven sisters
The numbers tell you it will be

The Numbers seven and three are key
Three bears, goats, and pigs you'll see
Before anyone can live happily

ever after

> Jenny Hartman-Tripp, Junior,
> Miami University

MEANINGFUL PLACES

In one of the Beatles' most poignant songs John Lennon sings about places he will remember all his life. We never forget that house, that neighborhood, that room.

Places shape us nationally, regionally, locally, even familially. My boyhood friend, for example, Ernesto Palleschi, was different from the rest of us in many ways. He had been born and raised in Sora, Italy, and came to Malvern, Ohio, at the beginning of his adolescence. Ern was fiercely independent, pragmatic, and decisive. He often did what we dreamed of doing. Ern was the third oldest among four brothers, all handsome, strong, and fearless. All of them but the youngest spoke with a slight Italian accent. Mr. and Mrs. Palleschi rarely spoke English at home. Ern's personality was partially shaped by place, both here in America and in the old country.

My relationship with my father is forever defined by the tavern and two bowling alleys he owned and operated when I was growing up. Fittingly enough for this section, my family referred to the business as *the place,* a working man's bar. We often called it something else:

> Ask students to write about a tangible thing or idea that is crucial in their subject's life. Deal with its specifics.

> Ask multigenre writers to identify places of importance in their topics and write about them. The Black Hills in a paper about Crazy Horse. Inside a Volkswagen bus in a paper about the Hippie era. And in a paper about Neil Armstrong, the moon.

The Beerjoint in Winter

I'm sweating hard from
baseball and July
when I step through the back
door of my dad's beerjoint.

It's 1959 and his is the only
air-conditioned business in town.
Cold air tightens my skin,
swirls around my wet neck
like the water last winter when I
skated fast over ice, tripped,
tumbled in midair, bashed
shoulder first through Sandy Creek.

In the dim beerjoint, a bee sound
rises from men walled at the bar.
They sip draft beer, lean toward
each other, talk, laugh.
Blue cigarette smoke floats above the hum.

My dad is an old-style bartender,
built this business twenty years ago.
A white apron falls to his knees,
is tied above his waist. He walks up to me,

reaches beneath the apron, pulls out a palm
brimming with silver coins.
I finger the edge of a quarter,
a half-dollar, pick the shiniest dime.
"Come back this afternoon," he says. "Fill
the coolers, go to the bank, burn the trash."

I nod, move behind the mahogany bar,
where Dad has worn a track in the tile floor.
I lean over the beverage cooler, slide back
the door, stick my sweaty head inside,
and shiver. Against a bottle of beer I press
my forehead, close my eyes, ache from the cold.

FIGURE 18–1.   *Philip Romano in his bar, circa 1941.*

19 | TEACHER EXPERTISE
Emotional Weight/ Informational Grounding

Some teachers have mentioned that some writers of research-based multi-genre papers unleash a flood of emotion with little factual information in it. Karen Blanchette spoke of one student who wrote about the migration of women westward: "Her entries were letters, journals, etc. that expressed pain and frustration but didn't give details." Sue Amendt echoed the problem. She has seen students focus "on the emotional too much with little background to allow the reader to understand the emotion."

Former journalist Don Murray (1993) contends that writers do not write with words; they write with information. "Readers read to satisfy their hunger for information—specific, accurate information they can use" (75).

Readers crave information. As writers we earn emotion with tangibles, with specific details of character and situation. "No ideas but in things," wrote poet William Carlos Williams (1985, 262).

In Chapter 4 I juxtaposed the encyclopedia entry with the poem about Count Basie and made a case for expanding our knowing beyond factual exposition to include narrative thinking and emotional content. I'm not backing off that. We need information, however, to understand the origins of emotion. The palpable is irreplaceable, the senses elemental. We need Basie's big feet beating the beat, his humped-back hulk at the piano, the "boogie woogie hordes burgeoning up from hell." In conferences, mini-lessons, and through our own writing we can show students the necessity of writing with pertinent information and senseful detail.

One of my students wrote a multigenre paper about a famous college football running back. The writer had played football himself in high school and college so he knew the sport from the inside. Even so,

> Before students write about some action or experience, have them take time to imagine it thoroughly—so thoroughly they reexperience it mentally. Ask them to jot down the sensory details of it. Give them time to talk about these details with a partner. Let language and senses merge. Fresh from that talking, move to writing.

he was having trouble writing with specific information. We spent time in conference talking about packing his writing with the tangibles he knew about playing football.

What was it physically like, I asked him, to carry the ball? What sensory stimulations bring the experience back?

He finally wrote about shifting his weight from the three-point stance, pushing off his right foot to cut in the backfield, the quarterback pressing the ball against his stomach, he covering the leather with his hand, his head low, eyes ahead, bodies roiling on the line of scrimmage before him, a hole opening, he plunging through it, linemen slapping at his pads as he blew by them to suddenly emerge in the open space of the defensive backfield.

After reading the detailed passage, I understood the thrill of the run.

Encourage your students to earn emotions with palpable information of both circumstance and senses.

20 | GENRES ANSWERED

One evening I talked long-distance to my mother about my father, Philip "Red" Romano. He has been dead thirty-six years, yet remains a presence in my life. I spoke to Mom about how distant he had been, his countless hours working in the bar and bowling alley, his inability to express affection. I never remember him kissing me. Nor my mother. Nor my sister. I told Mom about the one time I remember him physically punishing me. I was about nine and had arrived home hours after dark from sled riding. Mom was not home and dad whipped me with his belt. A few days after my conversation with Mom, I received this letter from her, she eighty-three then. I imagined her curving those crooked fingers around a pen and pouring out this urgent blend of memory and explanation:

May 15, 1998

Tommy, your Dad could never show his love by hugging or kissing. He showed it in so many other ways like he wanted an education so bad. He said his kids would get it, so he worked his ass off & took 4000 dollars in each of your names when you were born . . . the main thing was if you kids got sick, like the sled ride & getting home late. If you remember we had to eat at 5 P.M. every nite on the dot, so he could eat right away, take a 1/2 hr or 40 min nap then coffee & down to bowling alley or work. He was probably so flustered & worried about you. Then that time when you & John Savona played hookey, I got home from shopping & I parked in back of the place & Daddy came to the back door & yelled at me with his eyes brimming with tears & said Tommy's missing & go find him right now. I said Where will I go & he said Just get in the car & go. He really was terribly upset. I think the worst was when you were around 2 yrs old. Remember Antonia Recchio? Aunt Mary's Mother such a dear 4 ft little lady. Red always went to her for headaches. Any way you got very sick 1 eve. & Doc came around 11:00 at night & said you were a very sick little boy but he didn't know what was wrong & he would be back at 7 in the morn & have to take you to Little Flower hospital if you wasn't any better. Mary Markino & Daddy was there. After Doc left, Red said Mae I know you don't believe in this but if I go over & get Antonia & Mary said she is so good. Of course I said go. Antonia came right over & first she told me to get a bowl of water & olive oil & wanted me to go in your room & she would see if you had malocchio. I was afraid. I had never seen that so Mary & Red went in your room. & she said you didn't have malocchio so she told me to get a needle & thread & thread 9 pieces of garlic on it then Red & her went in your room & put it around your neck, then she came out to the kitchen & we all set in the booth & she told Red she would go home & it was up to Red in just a little while. He was to take the garlic off of Tom's neck & go out and bury & never tell any one where he buried it not even me & he never did . . . . Within the next hr you were completely well like nothing had happened. I guess Antonia prayed in Italian. Thats what your Aunt Mary said. When Doc came at 7, he said I can't understand it but Tommy is completely O.K. Red & I never said any thing. What faith that woman had. She would never take any thing would have been humbly-insulted. There was many times that Red just couldn't stand for you kids to get sick. As I'm writing this I can remember so many ways he showed his love. Tommy . . . it was Red's idea to take you to Fla. and let you eat Beef as much as you wanted I don't think you like Prime Rib a lot to this day. Another thing was teaching you to work at a very young age. This was a gift to you from your Dad so you would be independent & make your own way. He was very proud of you & Nancy. In trouble or out he was there for you. Just too hard for me to write.

Try to read between the lines Tom just can't write any more.

Mom's letter alerts me to this: Sometimes what we write needs to be answered. Sometimes the truth of one genre needs to be counterbalanced by the truth of another. In this case, the measured lines of my poem that end Chapter 18, the implicit presence of coldness, dimness, and distance in it are only part of the truth. Mom's letter reminds me of my father's determination that his children receive the college education he as an Italian immigrant in the early part of the twentieth century never came close to getting. She reminds me of my father's fierce, even harsh, loyalty and protection, his belief in the old ways—in Italian Catholic mysticism and a tiny Italian woman who cured headaches and sickness with olive oil, garlic, and prayer. Mom's letter reminds me that lives and love can be complicated. Easy, simplistic assessments are sure to miss complexity.

Sometimes—if we want to dig deeper in our multigenre papers, if we want to listen to all sides, to discover the unthought, the unperceived—

genres need to be answered. I'm glad I wrote "The Beerjoint in Winter." In a few words I got close to something true for me about place and my father's character. But I love Mom's letter, its detail, its love, its urgency, its sitting me down and not letting me go until I have heard her out and acknowledged other truths about the man she spent thirty years of her life with.

One piece of writing can play off another to explore further meaning. This was dramatically illustrated to me one evening in a graduate class. The culminating writing assignment of that course was to write a multigenre paper. In the weeks before the deadline, students paired up to lead the entire class in a writing activity. The pair could take the assignment anywhere it liked, just so the prompt enabled class members to turn the writing to their multigenre papers. My goal was threefold: to get students to practice theories and concepts we had been studying, to get them thinking and writing about their multigenre papers, and to experience the teaching talent of their peers. One evening two students showed the class effective leads from a number of writers. One example they used was the incredible opening of Carolyn Coman's novel *What Jamie Saw* (1995):

> When Jamie saw him throw the baby, saw Van throw the little baby, saw Van throw his little sister Nin, when Jamie saw Van throw his baby sister Nin, then they moved. (7)

After we had savored and discussed the various leads, talked about how these first words can lure readers or shut them down, the team asked us to create our own leads. Because of the Coman excerpt, rhythm and repetition were strong in me. I put a memory from adolescence on paper—betrayal, humiliation, and heartache all realized in one indelible moment:

> Saturday night. One in the morning. Under the street light on the square. Me. Sixteen. Dateless. My girl visiting her grandparents for the weekend. Snow sifting through the street light, landing dry on the pavement, the curb, the sidewalk, the Ford Galaxy pulled to a stop thirty yards in front of me, idling at the traffic light. That blonde head seated next to the driver, swiveling, that blonde head, black-framed glasses glinting, hair shiny and bright from the street light, that blonde head—the whole body really—rotating, seeming to rise up, looking away, wanting to crawl into the back seat, that blonde head so often on my shoulder, now pinned under the street light, snow falling lightly through the crisp February air, falling on the road, on the car, on me.

There isn't a complete sentence in any of those 132 words. Only sentence fragments, concrete detail, present participial phrases, and repeated images, yet for me they capture the feel and mood of that scene long ago. The next team that evening asked us to experiment with point of view. With excerpts from literature they demonstrated first person, second person, and third person. We discussed the limitations and strengths of each point of view, the gains and losses for the writer. When the team asked us to take ten minutes to write in a different point of view, I discovered that I wasn't done with Saturday night betrayal:

> We've just driven in from the lake where Gary and I parked on a hill and made out for an hour, on our way now to take me home, late, after one, so quiet and empty that the snow on the road has no tire tracks. The heater fan blasts warm air against my naked legs. I snuggle closer to Gary and he tightens his arm around my waist. As we approach the only traffic light in town, I see someone standing on the square, no hat, ears must be near frozen in the cold, and my breath catches because I realize how foolish it was to drive right up through the center of town—even this late—since that pathetic kid on the square could be a friend of Tom's—Sam or Danny or Ern—and all I would need is for him to recognize my blonde hair and tell Tom that I wasn't really out of town visiting my grandparents but God I had to tell Tom something, he's so clinging, so possessive. We head toward the light, now yellow. Gary taps the brake and as we roll to a stop, I get a clear look at the pathetic kid on the square and I want out of that car, out from under that street light. I turn my head quick and there is nowhere to go on the front seat of this Ford Galaxy and Gary is smiling, chuckling, saying three distinct words, "You . . . been . . . caught."

Exploring the experience through the girl's point of view—something I'd never done until that night in class—led me to perceive more deeply, to recognize things about myself at sixteen. My intellectual-emotional understanding of that indelible moment admitted a psychological element. I would argue that because of the "answer" to my first genre, the fullness of the experience on that Saturday night is rendered more deeply.

Have students review pieces they've created for their multigenre papers and look for

- a scene that could be rendered from another point of view
- a detail from a narrative or dialog that could be focused upon and exploded in a poem
- an incident that would benefit from two characters talking about it
- any piece that needs to be answered with countertruth

21 | EXPRESSIVE WRITING

Everyone who aspires to write ought to be adept at writing expressively. This includes seventh graders as well as graduate students. By *expressive* I do not mean *creative* or *emotional*. I mean *expressive* in the sense that James Britton used the word in *Language and Learning* (1970). In studying writing produced by British students eleven to eighteen years old, Britton and his colleagues identified three categories of writing: *poetic, transactional,* and *expressive*.

Poetic writing is what we often think of as creative writing—poems, stories, fables, plays, descriptions, etc. The idea is for readers to experience the writing, to be observers, to emotionally and intellectually give themselves over to the creation. The writing is important and valuable in and of itself, regardless of who reads it.

Transactional writing—by far the bulk of the writing scripts Britton collected—is writing to get some work of the world done. In the case of the British students, that work was almost entirely reports, essays, short answers. The students were trying to convince a teacher of something. The work of the world was to get a particular grade.

Transactional writing covers a broad range. Formal peace treaties between nations are transactional. So, too, are scribbled notes to a partner, reminding her to pick up rigatoni, anchovies, and olive oil at the grocery. Writers of transactional texts want someone to behave a certain way.

Expressive writing was the least-often used category. Expressive writing is personal and unpressured, relaxed and idiosyncratic. Code words and rhetorical shorthand communicate more meaning to the writer than they do to an outside audience. But then, expressive words aren't meant for an outside reader. We use expressive writing when we are trying to explain or render something for the first time, when we're seeking to recover information, make connections, generate ideas. Expressive writing is exploratory and new and focused on meaning. It might, therefore, be full of spelling errors, usage blunders, redundancies, incomplete scenes, partial thoughts, and faulty logic. That's OK; the writer is seeking to think on the page. At any time, of course, when writers have cut loose expressively, the writing might suddenly become poetic or transactional, the writer's voice and knowledge kicking in together, words popping on the page that work for an outside audience as well as the writer.

A journal or notebook or learning log is a perfect place for inexperienced writers to begin making forays with their expressive voices. In the journal they can name and describe and explain and dramatize, perhaps for the first time. During this act of unpressured composing, the more writers write, the more they remember. The more ideas unfold, the more writers know what they think. Many students, though, are impatient to get assignments done and turned in. They see time spent writing expressively as wasted. I lament that. Time spent writing expressively is anything but wasted.

When we write expressively in a journal, we imprint ideas, information, and experience deeply within us. We live topics by re-creating them with words on paper, by pulling images and dialog from the flow of our lives. With language we highlight the importance of something. In expressive writing—without fear of censure—we can easily blend fact, imagery, memory, and imagination. Just as novelists and biographers select and emphasize details for significance, so, too, does a journal writer who is bearing down to tell truth.

Expressive writing ought to be the rule for multigenre writers. Even when our goal is a polished poem or dialog, a fictional scene or a song, even a stream of consciousness, we ought to start by writing expressively, seeking the core of how we perceive and how we use language. Students can further let expressive writing work for them by keeping a learning log, journal, or sketchbook about their multigenre topics. Forget about genre and audience and balance and sources. Students use expressive writing to survey the terrain of their knowledge, to ramble about with language, to locate significant issues, and to pull to consciousness what they know but have forgotten.

When I taught high school seniors to write multigenre research papers, I asked them to turn in one thousand words a week of expressive writing in which they reported, conjectured, quoted, connected, created, experimented, even tried genres that seemed suddenly upon them. If students turned in the required amount of writing, they received full credit. A thousand words per week seemed enough to enable students to immerse themselves in language, to engage in sustained concentration, to surprise themselves during the meaning-making act of putting words on paper. Through expressive writing students can live the words of W. H. Auden: "Language is the mother, not the handmaiden, of thought; words will tell you things you never thought or felt before" (quoted in Murray 1978, 101).

Some multigenre teachers who also believe in the power of expressive writing have told me that one thousand words per week were more than their students could handle. Nanci Bush of Solon High School in Ohio, for example, thought that a five-hundred-word minimum was more appropriate for her students. I am reminded that always we have to adjust ideas and strategies to our own students and our own methods of working, all the while remaining theoretically grounded in sound practice. Helping students learn to unleash their expressive voices is sound practice in teaching writing. Such informal writing allows wide-ranging thought without pressure of product. It helps students prepare a rich, composted seedbed from which much can grow.

22 | IDENTITY, RACE, AND CLASSICAL LITERATURE

The author of this last multigenre paper was fifteen when she wrote "The Five Ages of Relationships" in Dorelle Malucci's Advanced Sophomore English class at Indian Hill High School in Cincinnati. As her students embarked on their multigenre projects, I visited Dorelle's class to help students identify indelible moments in their topics and to think about ways they might unify their papers. Later in the semester Dorelle sent me some of the students' papers. On subsequent visits to Indian Hill I met author Jacqui Copeland.

I was struck by Jacqui's straight posture, inquisitive eyes, and open face. She was a listener and also a talker. She enjoyed learning new words and trying them out on her friends and in her writing. When I asked Jacqui if she knew immediately what the topic of her paper would be, she said, "No, nobody did, because when Ms. Malucci is giving assignments, she's very nebulous."

Nebulous, I learned, was one of the class's vocabulary words that week.

Dorelle had framed the assignment this way: "In a multigenre paper write a portrait of yourself, choosing indelible moments from your past to create a sense of who you are."

One of the first writing assignments of the year, the multigenre paper had thrown many of the students into panic. Their previous experience with writing had been prescriptive and formulaic. The multigenre paper was a major leap.

To support them in developing their papers, Dorelle had students writing in "sketchbooks," an uninhibited place where they brainstormed, sketched, conjectured, and wrote expressively about indelible moments in their lives. "I started writing who I was in the sketchbook," said Jacqui. "The more I talked about it and wrote about it, I saw a focus appear—relationships with my family and friends."

There is another theme of "The Five Ages of Relationships." As Jacqui explored her experience in the sketchbook and paper, re-creating indelible moments in her life, working hard to make sense of them all, she confronted issues of race, culture, and identity.

Dorelle explained that the hardest thing for her sophomores was figuring out how to connect genres. Jacqui wondered about this, too. She discovered a suitable form, though, when passion for her topic combined with the famous speech of Jacques from *As You Like It* and the literary device of the *chorus* in Greek tragedy. Human invention never ceases to delight me. Jacqui didn't study classical literature merely to attain cultural literacy or to prepare for an advanced placement test. She developed a personal relationship with it. She connected form and meaning to her personal life and used the classical texts to launch her own postmodern writing.

THE FIVE AGES OF RELATIONSHIPS

September 21, 1998

Dear Reader,

As this assignment began, I found myself falling into the same old track of other assignments. I was writing in order to give the teacher what I felt she wanted to hear. In this, I would have found contentment. However, somewhere between my first draft and my sketchbook I found that this paper would require more effort than I had believed. I realized two facts: one, that writing about myself would require as much research as any other paper, if not more. Secondly, to accomplish this paper I would actually need to think of who I was rather than give the teacher what I thought she might enjoy as me. Therefore, I sat down with my sketchbook and then later, I sat down with my sketchbook and my mother, in order to discover me. From there, the piece flowed together; what I wanted to convey merged with how I wanted to convey it. I saw the important role relationships played in my development. I also saw how past relationships have affected me and together I saw how relationships formed who I am today.

I decided to try again and took my pencil into hand. The result consisted of me upon paper. I was pleased to find that the imaginary self had disappeared.

While talking to my mom I remembered a poem that our class read in ninth grade called the "Seven Ages of Man." This poem reminded me greatly of what my paper was shaping into, hence, the title of my paper and the titles within my paper evolved. Also, I felt that to accomplish this piece I had to find a structure that went along with the title. Conveniently, my Latin class began to study Greek tragedies. I found that to approach my paper in the similar structure of a Greek tragedy would offer uniqueness as well as a continuation of Shakespeare's idea. I fully understood the paper when finally all these ideas came together. Ms. Malucci, I thank you for this piece, which no longer floats in space.

Sincerely,

Jacqui Copeland

"All the world's a stage. / And all the men and women merely players; / They have their exits and their entrances; / And one man in his time plays many parts" "The Seven Ages of Man" by William Shakespeare

Act 1: "At first the infant."

They embraced me—when I never asked.
My tears brushed away—before they fell.
Tickled, played with, grinned at—when I did not understand.

My cries always answered, silenced—before they were heard.
Oblivious, content, indulged—when my feelings could not matter.
Loved—when I never asked.

All this then
Was taken, never given.
Yet it was unselfish,
a baby taking love and never giving.
For there was so little love for me to give.

When I could not talk—
When I could not disagree—
When I could not walk away—

CHORUS——THE PARENTS

Embraced	
With love.	With love.
We bought you	We bought you
	Matching underwear and socks, the
	Kind with ruffles,
Which you couldn't	Which you couldn't
Help but to show off.	
We drove you around at	
Night	
	To put you to sleep
With you our hearts	With you our hearts
Melded together	Melded together
	We worked day

And night.
To provide you
With everything
You needed.

So oblivious and content

We loved you before you
Asked for love.
So much of us

Your stubbornness

So little to love
Yet we loved you so much.

To provide you
With everything

To show our love.

We indulged your every wish.
We loved you before you
Asked for love.

Showed through you.

Your patience,
So little to love
Yet we loved you so much.

ACT 2: "And then the whining schoolboy"

*Running . . . running . . . screams that escaped and engulfed the room . . .
screams of trepidation, of confusion . . . ubiquitous chaos . . . running . . .
running . . . scalding tears and seething anger . . . the children stood
with silent stares of disbelief etched upon their faces . . .*

*She ran—searching for something—perhaps the embrace of loving
arms—yet she ran—as though her existence depended upon her escape—
her heart thundered with fear—and the tears showered from her eyes—
creating a different view of the children, the teachers, the classroom
around her—confusion surrounding her—closing in . . . running . . .
with no time to think.*

*Sanity in those few moments did not exist within her—already lost—
finding strength no one knew she embodied—a voice her small being
could not possess—all around her—all against her—she knew only that
she could not allow them to possess her as they tried now to do.*

*Huddled in a corner now—no longer running—scalding tears still
ravaging down her cheeks—seething anger still constricting her chest—
tidal waves of confusion rocking over her brain—she still and always
held the control.*

CHORUS—THE TEACHERS

We tried to calm her.
But it was as though
Her sanity—

Such rage—

All from a small child.
Screaming.

We tried to calm her.

Gone

—An animal
All from a small child.
Screaming.

Fighting us
As though we—

Scared—the whole
Classroom—petrified.

No one!
Attempt what?
Embrace that child?
Her?

Beyond mine as well.

I knew only this:
That child needed
Help.

Fighting us
As though we—
Monsters.

Of this disturbed child
No one could control!
No one!

Her?
Beyond my call of duty—

For I recognized only one thing:

That child needed
Help.

Act 3: "And then the justice"

N———. The one taboo word in our society whose meaning each African-American child learns at a far too young age. In a world where racial tension grows with each passing minute, it surprises no one that in a small catholic school the taboo word finds its way into the ears of each black child.

Take an African-American child in a white environment, forced to grow and develop here, her friends consist of the white children that surround her. The most detrimental event in her young life will occur when one of her "friends" calls her the one word that never is said. Imagine when not one of her friends understands fully what she feels when the word escapes another supposed friend's mouth. Like a bucket of ice cold water, realization hits that her friends view her differently than their other friends, she being black. To think that all this time— tricked—into believing you are seen equally.

Everyday this realization hits another small African-American child, helping her realize that what she thought true of her relationships with her peers only turns out as a convincing facade. Those friends, of course, never realize the full extent of their beliefs, feelings, and thoughts in saying that one taboo word. However, this small black child knows all in that moment, even as all she has ever known crumbles before her eyes.

Equal what?

As equal.
That's ridiculous.
When we—so obviously—

Besides—we are

Look at that hair.
So tight and kinky.
Why not beautiful like ours.

DIFFERENT.
And the color of your skin.

Not my fault
That you want eyes
Like mine.
Your stance—
Even DIFFERENT.
Yet you find it hard to believe
That accepting
Is what we find taboo.

Expected of us to see you
As equal.

DIFFERENT.
Embracing other cultures.
We just don't do well.

DIFFERENT.

Your nose,
Compared to mine's—

You talk, dress, act besides so
. . . Differently.

Like mine.
Your stance—
Even DIFFERENT.

That accepting
Is what we find taboo.

Act 4: "Then the soldier"

"Are those butterflies in my stomach?"

Why would you contain butterflies in your stomach. Your event is a couple of hours away.

"Well, I'm warming up."

And? So what?

"Okay, it is not the race. I guess these black people that surround me make the butterflies appear. I don't want to look stupid. I want to look cool. Not like some geek that goes to a private school."

You do go to a private school, but I guess I see the problem.

"Yeah, I figured you would."

Get more practice, hang out with black kids more. Then when you get to these blistering hot things they call track meets—no problems.

"Easier said than done. Remember, I go to an all white school."

Oh, you would use that as an excuse for not having enough black friends to feel comfortable around the ones you don't know.

"It's not an excuse, and it's not that I don't feel comfortable around them exactly . . ."

Sure. Then what? Let me hear this one.

"Well, I just feel as if I need to make a good impression on them. You know, be cool, talk cool, act cool. You know—act black."

How can you act black, fool?

"Okay, relate to black. Same thing. Just have something in common with them, know all the words."

All right. I will give you that one. If you talk in your regular voice—that valley girl one—shoot, I would not accept you as part of my culture either. Yet, you do know some stuff. Just go up to one of them. Say hi. If all these black kids can talk to each other as if they have known each other for years instead of one day, surely you can muster up enough guts to do the same.

"Easier said than done. I'm not used to doing this with black kids. I barely know how they will react."

Well, you want to become friends with them, don't you?

"Sure."

Then go up to one of them.

"See, this is the cause of my butterflies."

CHORUS—THE RUNNERS

Look at that girl.

        Which one?

The one over there.
Now who does she think
She is.

        Yeah, I know.
        Tried talking to her yesterday.

I wonder if she
Knows how?

        How what?
To hold a conversation.
        To hold a conversation?
        I doubt it.

Why doesn't she just
Talk.

        Talk.
        She looks as if she could use
        A friend.

Standing alone.

        Perhaps nervous?
Her event—hours away.
        Her event—hours away.
Perhaps afraid?
Of what though?
        Of what though?
Of looking stupid?

        No—acting stupid.

Talking stupid?
Perhaps.
Who knows?

Who cares?

Besides, my event—
NEXT!

Besides, my event—
NEXT!

Act 5: "Pantaloon"

What's up, Grecia and Faith,

I just wanted to thank you for helping me mature and grow. If you are laughing as you read this, I understand why. Before I entered Indian Hill High School, I was confused. Confusion centered around my relationships with others, especially friends. All my friendships up to this point were shallow. Upon coming to Indian Hill, however, I found you both and with you I found "enlightenment," a new quality of friendship. Unfortunately, as a child, I did not understand my friends from Summit nor my relationships with them. I also did not possess many black friends. This left me alone and frustrated. Then I found you both and upon this discovery I met myself; eccentric and romantic, intellectual and naive—I realized me. I also realized all the black friends I had and made two more. I finally knew of what true friendship consists. Black friends never exclude you, never make a racially hurtful statement about you, and understand what it feels like to have another student call you a n———. No matter how good of a friend a person of another race is, they simply do not understand our blackness.

However, this makes up only the smallest piece of what I discover everyday. I never realized how much I enjoy partying, meeting new people, and love boys. In your company I learn more about me. I have learned how to balance relationships with other races, and learned that if they hurt me, it is only a result of their not understanding me fully. Now, I know true friendships. All this results from finding you both and so I thank you, for accepting me, for finding me.

Best Friends Forever And Ever,

Jacqui

Now, when I am older
No longer a small toy that fits the predefined mold.
When I can talk—
When I can disagree—
When I can walk away—

Love, willingly handed over and taken equally,
For to take and not give is selfish.
When there is more to love.

I know this now.

23 | UNITY AND FULFILLMENT

Recently I shared my students' multigenre work at John Carroll University in Cleveland with a positive, upbeat group of college and high school teachers. At one point I talked about the major problem I find in students' multigenre papers: an absence of unity.

"Why," one participant asked, "are you concerned about something so traditional as unity when multigenre papers break so many rules of traditional composition?"

I froze, caught like a deer in the beam of his incisive question, then blurted: "Because I want to understand them."

Multigenre papers require a great deal of readers. So much is implicit, so little explicit that multigenre papers can be quite a cognitive load. Because they can be so demanding to read and because they lack traditional transitions found in regular research papers, I nudge students to provide recurring images, echoes of language, and repetition of form that reverberate among genres. In Chapter 20 my mother's letter in defense of my father—in addition to answering my poem with a countertruth—adds unity to my understanding. And this I find fulfilling. Unforgettable people move through our lives, people we haven't seen in years, even those who are dead, often long dead. Events connect, images recur, words repeat, themes emerge.

One clear lesson I learned from Michael Ondaatje was how skillful repetition can add unity to multigenre writing.

FRAGMENTING THE STORY

Not far into *The Collected Works of Billy the Kid* (1970) the reader turns a page and is shocked by a brief, first-person poem that begins, "When I caught Charlie Bowdre dying . . . ." Bowdre is part of Billy's gang. We have no context for this terrible moment of fifty-three words, when Bowdre is suddenly shot and thrown backwards, crying out,

o my god
o my god billy I'm pissing watch
your hands (12)

The sound of voices is strong in these eight lines: Billy's vivid, matter-of-fact description, Bowdre's whimpering, embarrassed warning. As strong as the voices, however, is the visual image of Bowdre shot, flying backwards "in a gaggle," frantically warning his friend of the mess "while the eyes grew over his body." (Those growing eyes I take to mean bullet wounds seeping blood.) Despite the vivid sharpness of voice and image, the brief scene is a puzzle—no context, no warning. How does the shooting of Bowdre fit? What does it mean in the larger context of the story?

Ten pages later in a brief narrative Billy sets the scene at Tivan Arroyo, also called Stinking Springs, where he and three of his gang members have passed the night in a cabin. In the morning Bowdre rises to fetch wood and feed the horses. One step out the door and he is shot, the impact burning the clothes off his stomach, lifting "him right back into the room." Billy knows Bowdre is dying and urges him out the door to go down shooting. Charlie says, "No Billy. I'm tired, please. Jesus watch your hands Billy."

Lights of understanding blaze for readers. We hear the echo of Charlie's first warning in the poem. We understand how it fits. With intensity we read the rest of the narrative, learn of Charlie dying without another shot fired, observe Sheriff Pat Garrett's coolness, get a sense of this "academic murderer." The passage ends with these lines:

> Snow outside. Wilson, Dave Rudabaugh and me. No windows, the door open so we could see. Four horses outside. (22)

For twenty-five pages after this shocking, matter-of-fact scene, Ondaatje—often through Billy's voice but sometimes through the voices of others and sometimes through an omniscient third-person narrator—introduces us to more characters and their relationships, presents incisive sketches of Pat Garrett and Sallie Chisom, brief philosophical asides, stories revealing life and times, narratives depicting debauchery and violence. Then we come upon this paragraph on a page by itself:

> Snow outside. Wilson, Dave Rudabaugh and me. No windows, the door open so we could see. Four horses outside. Garrett aimed and shot to sever the horse reigns. He did that for 3 of them so they got away and 3 of us couldn't escape. He tried for 5 minutes to get the reigns on the last horse but kept missing. So he shot the horse. We came out. No guns. (48)

Since twenty-five pages and much information have passed since that startling poem that begins the ambush of the Kid's gang in the cabin at Stinking Springs, Ondaatje cues readers' understanding and orientation by repeating *snow, four horses,* and the names of characters. We learn of Garrett's brutal pragmatism, the gang's hopeless situation, and the scene's denouement—their surrender.

Ondaatje achieves unity in the first half of *The Collected Works of Billy the Kid* through repetition of imagery and language, through fragmenting this pivotal story of Billy the Kid's surrender, strategically placing those fragmented parts for maximum impact. As a reader I am rewarded and fulfilled by the flashes of recognition, the building of meaning, and the familiar echoes of word and image.

EXTENDING THE STORY

On two occasions I have read devastating multigenre papers about eating disorders. Kirsten's paper that I excerpted a mother's journal entry from in Chapter 12 was compassionate and outraged and arose from considerable academic research into the subject and her observation of a close friend. Leah Burge, a young high school teacher, took another route. In her multigenre paper she rendered what it felt like from the inside to have an eating disorder. In her note to the reader, Leah wrote,

> This paper is not meant to teach you about eating disorders. Everyone who experiences anorexia or bulimia goes through something different . . . . What I want you to see is how this disease affected one person. Me.

Leah takes us through her own journey, using narratives, poems, reflective essays, dialog, descriptive passages, and—throughout her paper, just as they occur throughout our culture—photos of advertisements and models, headlines and sidebars she's cut from mainstream magazines that illustrate the popular culture's view of women, romance, and sex. On the second page of her paper Leah writes a stream of consciousness titled

the toilet

why am i eating i can't believe i had the nerve to order it i know she knows these are my favorite but they are so fattening i don't even like anything else on the menu or anything that is healthy that fry looks so good i wonder if she finds it strange that i dip everything into honey mustard sauce i love it i wish they sold it in stores no because then i would eat it all the time i am eating too quickly slow down cut it up move it around more pop yet another refill please pop makes the hunger go away so i can feel the gurgle in my stomach the diet pepsi wish washing around in my empty canyon of a stomach god i feel full i bet my yep it is sticking out all right i don't really need to suck it in here though no one can see anyway maybe i should just go to the bathroom i haven't seen anyone walk that way for a long time that kind of sucks though because then someone is more than likely to walk in screw it i'll go

Following this stream of consciousness inside the head of a young woman with an eating disorder, Leah writes a description of the indelible moment in a college dining hall when she made the choice to reject a full meal in favor of a light one. She follows this with an incisive rhyming poem about the way fat distributes when the legs are crossed carefully, a free-verse poem about awakening in the morning and immediately probing the skin of her stomach and thigh for fat deposits, and a reflective narrative about the central act in her life of *lying*—to her friends, her boyfriend, her parents, herself. Then, surprisingly, with the next piece we are back in a familiar place, going where we might not want to go but where Leah must take us:

the toilet—continued

shut the door pull back your hair first you have to insert your finger in your mouth to get it wet rub it over your teeth because that feels good now give yourself a few baby pokes get your stomach ready for what is about to come but this makes you cough no one is in here though so who cares a few more little pokes there you go now lean over and way down the smell of disinfectant is staring at me it is so degrading to be this close to the seat of a toilet in a public place i wonder how many germs are resting there right now ok the final plunge pull your finger out quickly it comes out fast furious again again again stop no when it comes through your nose you are doing it too much take the toilet paper wipe your finger off now blow your nose and feel the chunks of chicken try to squeeze their way out of your skinny nostrils flush the toilet but wait to make sure everything goes down will mary know what i have been doing watery eyes scratchy voice and throat maybe but probably not

Students are often drawn to big, important topics when they write multigenre papers. Leah was no exception. Her topic was crucial to her very life. In an assessment of her work, Leah wrote,

> I really enjoyed writing the multigenre paper. We were allowed to explore, dream, imagine, and interpret our world, others, and society. Although it was really difficult for me, the paper represents where I am right now and I know (or hope) that some day I will be able to look back on it in amazement. The best thing for me about this paper is that it is a work-in-progress. Many of these issues or topics are still very unclear to me. But as I grow I want to keep a record of my progress and I think this is the perfect starting point.

Leah told me several times how difficult it was for her to share this particular work with peers, especially one week when we switched groups so that people had a chance to confer with others in the class. I kept encouraging Leah to write what she needed to write. Sharing and conferring were important parts of class, but they were not as important as writing what mattered. I often tell people who write in my workshops and classes to keep "faith" and "fearlessness." Faith that language resides in them and fearlessness in following that language to speak the best and hardest truths they can. Leah had plenty of both.

PACING REPETITION

During one semester a close family friend of one of my students died suddenly of a heart attack at forty-six years old. Brooke decided to write a multigenre paper about "Buster"; she would reveal his character through his relationships with others. Near the end of her paper, Brooke renders a moment that had become part of the folklore surrounding her family's relationship with Buster.

The Making of a Legend

"Why is she crying. She never cries. She loves us." Buster stands over the play pen making faces at the baby.

"She's a baby and she's tired," Debbie says. "Let her go to sleep. She'll be fine."

"I don't think she needs to go to bed yet. She just got here. We need to play with her a little bit first."

Buster hangs over the edge of the play pen and dances various toys in front of the whimpering child. "How's our favorite baby?" Buster picks her up and throws her into the air. The baby giggles and he throws her into the air again and again. The baby begins to fuss.

"I'm telling you, just lay her down with her blanket and she falls asleep. Leave her alone. We can play with her tomorrow and she'll be her normal, pleasant self." Debbie turns her back to the multicolored quilt.

Buster continues to try to make the baby laugh, bouncing her up and down on his knee. She enjoys it for a few minutes then starts fussing again.

"I've got it! Do you want to play with my favorite hat? I know you do. You love my hat. Here you go." Buster hands the baby his favorite, beat up old hat.

The baby coos at the sight of the old thing, picks it up, turns it over, and spits up in it.

Buster stares at the mess incredulously. "She just puked in my favorite hat!"

"I told you to let her go to sleep, but you had to keep shaking her up. It's no wonder she spit up. Now, will you let her go to sleep?"

"I'm never going to let her forget about this one. That was my favorite hat."

10 years later . . . .

"I just wanted her to stop crying, so I jiggled her around a little bit. You know, tossed her up in the air, bounced her around on my knee. She loved it. Then I let her play with my favorite hat and she threw up in it."

15 years later . . . .

"I was just trying to get her to go to sleep. She wanted to stay up and play so she was crying. I thought I'd let her play with my favorite hat. That was the only thing that would stop her from crying, and Brooke here, threw up in it."

20 years later . . . .

"For some reason she just loved my very favorite hat. Brooke was spending the night with us and I was trying to put her to bed, when she grabbed my hat off the top of my head and just turned it over and puked in it!"

Brooke Maynard, Junior,
Miami University

I understood Buster's exuberance and insistence. I saw the slight ways the story changed so that he exonerated himself of all blame and made Baby Brooke appear willful and mischievous. All this happens on a page, effectively, I think. Another way Brooke could have revealed this information, however, is more slowly, using the thematic thread contained in the story to add unity and fulfillment. Brooke might have placed the opening narrative early in her paper, and then strategically throughout the remainder of it she might have placed the different parts of Buster's monolog that reveal the story's transformation.

REPETEND

In *An Alternate Style: Options in Composition,* Winston Weathers writes about a rhetorical device called the *repetend.* The way I understand *repetend,* it is the unexpected repetition of a word, phrase, sentence, or passage (Romano 1995a, 80). Unlike the regular appearance of a refrain, the repetend gains power and impact by its unexpected use.

Take a look (and a listen) at Joan Didion's repetition of key words and parallel sentence patterns in a New Journalism piece titled "The White Album" (1979). She writes about a quintessential 1960s rock band, The Doors, and its visionary, self-destructive lead singer:

On this evening in 1968 . . . [t]here was everything and everybody The Doors needed to cut the rest of this third album except one thing, the fourth Door, the lead singer, Jim Morrison, a 24-year-old graduate of U.C.L.A. who wore black vinyl pants and no underwear and tended to suggest some range of the possible just beyond a suicide pact. It was Morrison who had described The Doors as "erotic politicians." It was Morrison who had defined the group's interests as "anything about revolt, disorder, chaos, about activity that appears to have no meaning." It was Morrison who got arrested in Miami in December of 1967 for giving an "indecent" performance. It was Morrison who wrote most of The Doors' lyrics, the peculiar character of which was to reflect either an ambiguous paranoia or a quite unambiguous insistence upon the love-death as the ultimate high. And it was Morrison who was missing. It was Ray Manzarek and Robby Krieger and John Densmore who made The Doors sound the way they sounded, and maybe it was Manzarek and Krieger and Densmore who made seventeen out of twenty interviewees on *American Bandstand* prefer The Doors over all other bands, but it was Morrison who got up there in his black vinyl pants with no underwear and projected the idea, and it was Morrison they were waiting for now. (23)

I've never owned black vinyl pants and I've always worn underwear. Nevertheless, when Didion repeats those details in the final sentence after introducing them two hundred words earlier and building momentum with the succession of sentences that begin with "It was," I am rewarded and feel like an insider. I understand something of Morrison's boldness, juvenality, and counterculture pretense. The repetend of Morrison's vinyl fashion sense is an emotional payoff, a stimulating intellectual burst of familiarity.

When I wrote Chapter 11 of *Clearing the Way* (1987) years ago, I was in the throes of reading New Journalism and studying Winston Weather's *An Alternate Style*. Repetition of key words, ebullience of language, and sense of risk and abandon were in my bones. Here is the lead to "Literary Warnings," the chapter Don Murray said I wrote to beat up on literature professors:

That brilliant professor who taught you modern-Victorian-Romantic-Shakespearean-critical approaches to literature may well have been your worst writing teacher. I know—I've just raised your hackles. After all, that brilliant professor provided the inspiration that propelled you into teaching. Every class meeting was a tour de force in literary exegesis, a stimulating hour of one mind succinctly unfolding a critical analysis of the work under study, weaving together and testing the validity of years of prominent literary research.

Remember the intricate analysis of the symbolism in *The Sun Also Rises*? The meticulous explication of every allusion in "The Waste Land"? The fascinating Freudian interpretation of *Alice's Adventures in Wonderland*? Remember how raptly you listened, how fervidly you wrote notes? Remember how that brilliant professor's insights burst in your mind like fireworks, how he drew everything together so you could begin to truly appreciate . . . what? Novels? Poetry? Plays? Essays?

No. That brilliant professor of literature taught you to appreciate, uphold, and revere high-grade, premium, hard-to-come-by, top-of-the-line literary art.

And you did. You did.

But, I repeat, that brilliant professor may have been your worst writing teacher . . . . (163–64)

THE REPETEND OF ARTISTRY

After reading *The Collected Works of Billy the Kid,* I read Michael Ondaatje's other books. One of my favorites was *Coming Through Slaughter* (1976), a novel based on the life of Buddy Bolden, a jazz coronetist in New Orleans in the early 1900s. At thirty-one he suffered a mental breakdown and was soon committed to a pre–Civil War asylum where he spent the last twenty-four years of his life and was abused, raped, and isolated. Although for many of those years of institutionalization he barbered—his day job before psychologically coming apart—he never played the coronet again.

Think of that. He never again blew jazz, never again performed that act that was the grand passion of his life. Ondaatje explores the interior lives of Bolden and those who surrounded him, expanding and polishing historical fact to "suit the truth of fiction" (Ondaatje 1976, credits). In this story of genius, passion, madness, and tragedy, Ondaatje employs a repetend that confounded me initially and ultimately stunned me with the implications that reverberated from its final use.

Sixty pages into this postmodern novel, the fragmented narrative is broken further by a page with only one line on it:

Passing wet chicory that lies in the field like the sky.

I puzzled over this unexpected poetic image, struggling to see the sense of it, unable to connect it with what had come before or what appeared on the next page. One thing was sure, though: its startling appearance remained steadfast in my subconscious. Twenty-five pages later, after Bolden's occasional bizarre behavior is revealed and his sudden disappearance occurs, I came to another confounding page: a poem in which the chicory line is repeated twice, followed by five lines using variations of its exact language. This poem consolidates the image, imprints on the reader the significance of *wet chicory, sky,* and *passing.* But still no meaningful understanding came to me beyond the belief that if Ondaatje were repeating the image, it must be important.

I read on and learned of the search for Bolden and his return to New Orleans two years later to find his wife living with a musician friend. No rage from Bolden, though. After all, he was the one who disappeared and for two years made no contact with wife, children, friends, or professional associates. Once returned, however, Bolden blended into his former life. Then Ondaatje bends reality to suit the truth of fiction again—in a parade through the streets of New Orleans, Bolden suffers a dramatic physical and mental breakdown. The way Ondaatje renders the scene, the irony is almost too tragic to bear. At the moment of mental slippage, Bolden has perfectly merged art and life, is absolutely one with his coronet, "hitting slow pure notes." But at the moment his mind is exploding, his very blood was rising up in him, filling the horn (130–31).

His life of loving and creativity and freedom end. Two months later two civil sheriffs escort him, hands bound, by train and by wagon to the East Louisiana State Hospital. On the train Bolden looks out the window on the last day he will ever spend outside an institution. He observes the train "passing wet chicory that lies in the field like the sky" (139). And now I know why the image is crucial. It is freedom. It is poetry. It is art. It is perception in the big wide world. It is everything opposite the mean existence Bolden learned to live for twenty-four years in the insane asylum until the day he died.

Michael Ondaatje had employed perhaps the purest form of *repetend*. It is poetic and subtle, risking enigma and the kind of frustration that makes readers stop reading. But the final use of the repetend is a payoff clear and profound.

REPETEND OF FORM

In a multigenre paper titled "Poetry Can Be . . ." undergraduate Suzi Kelly explored the kinds of poetry someone might write, the many ways that writing poetry can please and satisfy. Before she got into her heavy, confessional free-verse poetry, Suzi included this poem near the beginning of her paper:

A Little Fun Never Hurt Anyone

Rhyme, Shmime
All the time.
Greeting cards do it.
Songs stick to it.
What about you?
Do you do it too?

Me—I hate it.
Won't debate it.
Rhyming sucks

Like ugly ducks.
Rhyming stinks
Like sweaty rinks.
Rhyming bites
Like broken kites.

Gee, this is fun.
It's fun a ton.
I like to rhyme.
Do it all the time.
I know I'm dense.
I'm on the fence.

So rhyme away.
Rhyme all day.
Have fun with rhyme.
It's not a crime.
Just don't go crazy
Or you'll be a . . . daisy?

Me: Ya, know, that kinda reminds me of
Dr. Suess. He was cool.
Me too: He sure was.

Suzi Kelly, Junior,
Miami University

Suzi enjoys the fun of rhyming and, at the same time, implicitly points out in her last two lines the dilemma of diction and meaning that using a rhyme scheme sometimes creates. Despite the fun of the poem, however, look to the bottom of it, where she employs two voices: "Me" and "Me too." Three times in her brief multigenre paper, Suzi uses the two voices, the two halves of herself that are usually at odds, even though here they agree that Dr. Suess was, indeed, cool. The "me" voice, we learn, is bold and venturesome; the "me too" voice is cautious and worrisome. Always occurring together in that dialog form, the "voices" have a unifying effect in the paper. I found it pleasurable to encounter them.

To unify their papers and emphasize important acts or images, some of my students—like Suzi—have repeated a form instead of the exact words of a line. Brian McKnight's poem "Unfinished Music #1," which appears in Chapter 7, was one of three poems about the shooting of John Lennon, all of them using *Unfinished Music* in the title. Fourth-grade teacher Charlene Dunn of Salt Lake City wrote a multigenre paper about music, the abiding passion of her life, particularly her own singing. Eight pages into her paper she used the voice of her strong-willed, autocratic, and beloved vocal teacher to isolate an important concept of singing:

Support!
Support with your diaphragm
let the sound float
    past your throat
    to your head

Fill the air chambers
    in your head
    with sound

Let sound resonate
    behind
    the mask
    of your face

Eight pages following the first lesson readers nod familiarly as Charlene continues the form and refines the lesson:

Lessons - # 2

Sing through the mask
Let it resonate through your head
Don't punch it!
    Delicate,
    Delicate,
Let it light like a bird on a branch.

                Charlene Dunn, Teacher,
          Beacon Hights Elementary School

Vicki Scott, teacher and language arts consultant, worked in Lindley Weygandt's classroom at Batesville High School in Arkansas, teaching seniors to write multigenre papers. One student, Kelly Rigby, wrote a perceptive paper about Marilyn Monroe. Kelly invented a form that she varied and repeated throughout her paper. She began with the title of a Monroe film, followed it with the genre, then concluded with an ironic, prophetic, or summative quotation from Monroe. Alternating with photographs, fifteen of these genres appear. Here is one that even varies the pattern Kelly has set up:

Gentlemen Prefer Blondes

Marilyn is gorgeous
    forgiving
    the child-woman
    humorous
    compliant
    sexy
    tender
    personifies all my secret hopes
    GODDESS.

"My popularity seemed almost a masculine phenomenon."

> Marilyn is flirty
> a man stealer
> too blonde
> too giving
> too vulnerable
> personifies all my fears
> I can't compete
> TRAMP.

"I have always had a talent for irritating women since I was fourteen."
Kelly Rigby, Senior,
Batesville High School

Your students might find that creating a repetend of some sort to unify their papers will prove meaningful, depending upon the tone they are trying to create. Smart, clever, and critical like Joan Didion. Poetic and tragic like Michael Ondaatje. Playful and assured like Suzi Kelly.

LAST WORDS ON REPETITION

One Friday night my wife and I went to see *Mr. Holland's Opus* (1995), the title role played by Richard Dreyfuss. What a night for me . . . acting, directing, music, and writing all combining to bowl me over as I experienced the growth and learning, the disappointments and triumphs, of Glen Holland's life. So taken was I with the film that the following evening when Kathy was working, I went by myself to see it again. Mr. Holland was a music teacher, but so much of what he experienced and learned resonated in me, a writing teacher. Another aspect of the film I admired was its structure—so much like a multigenre paper—with self-contained, revelatory sequences spanning a thirty-year period and an effective and evocative use of repetition by screenwriter Patrick Duncan and director Stephen Herek.

As a beginning teacher Mr. Holland is full of himself and his discipline. He considers teaching a fallback job he'll do only long enough until he can resume a professional music career. It is no surprise that he is not a good teacher. Initially, he is overwhelmed and disillusioned, then he grows impatient as his students appreciate music narrowly and play their instruments poorly. Mr. Holland responds with superiority and disdain. He arrogantly propounds music theory and technique and ridicules students in class for their ignorance and naiveté. Under Mr. Holland's direction, even students who love music learn to loathe it.

Principal Jacobs, played by Olympia Dukakis, is clear-eyed, acerbic, and straight-talking. At the end of one school day four or five months into the year, she catches Mr. Holland in the hallway and asks him to serve on a committee. He, of course, declines. Jacobs decides to speak her mind: "I've never seen a teacher sprint for the parking lot after last period with more speed and enthusiasm than his students. Perhaps you should be our track coach."

Mr. Holland is quick to counter: "I get here on time every morning, don't I? I'm doing my job the best I can."

"A teacher is two jobs," says Mrs. Jacobs. "Fill young minds with knowledge, yes. What's more important, give those minds a compass so that that knowledge doesn't go to waste. Now, I don't know what you're doing with the knowledge, Mr. Holland, but as a compass, you're stuck."

Mr. Holland begins to examine his teaching, concluding that his positive impact has been zero. He realizes that to teach effectively he must connect with students, must help them connect with music—any music—regardless of where they are in their musical development. He begins to help students to their *own* understanding and accomplishment.

Years later, during the festivities of graduation day, Mrs. Jacobs takes Mr. Holland aside and tells him she has decided to retire. She gives him a momento of their work together.

The director uses an extreme close-up to reveal what Mr. Holland sees when he opens the present: an elegant, gold-plated compass.

Even the third time I saw the film, I caught my breath. The unexpected repetition of the idea through image was superb writing. Words were unnecessary as character and meaning coalesced in one profoundly affecting moment.

Students, too, can employ repetition in sophisticated ways. Linda Cunningham, a business teacher at Salt Lake Community College and a master's degree student when I met her at Utah State University, wrote a multigenre paper spurred by Mary Crow Dog's *Lakota Woman* (1990) and further research into the American Indian Movement (AIM) of the 1970s. In the second encounter at Wounded Knee, South Dakota, between federal troops and Sioux Indians, Mary Crow Dog is the Lakota woman who gives birth during the siege. At Wounded Knee Mary came to know Annie Mae Aquash. On one page Linda features a monolog by Mary Crow Dog, the first time we learn of Annie:

> Annie Mae Aquash became my best friend at Wounded Knee—and afterward. She was a Micmac Indian from Nova Scotia. Like so many of us, her life had been physically and emotionally hard. Being cold, hungry and poor was about the only thing she could count on as a kid. Annie was beautiful and energetic, so she left home when she was 17 to make her way in the big city—Boston. She met up with AIM on the east coast and helped them bury Plymouth Rock under a truckload of sand as a protest.
>
> Annie came . . . [west] after the eastern protests as AIM shifted its focus to the Sioux reservations in South Dakota where the elders still observed the traditional Indian ceremonies. The Micmac had lost almost all of their traditions, and Annie wanted to learn the ancient ways so that she could take them to her people.

During the 71 days at Wounded Knee, we became close. . . . We talked about our early lives and the paths our feet had walked to bring us to that place. Although we couldn't have said why at the time, we both knew that Wounded Knee would have a profound effect on our lives—and it has.

On the following page Linda includes a poem she has written about some of the things that happened at Wounded Knee between the Sioux and the massive assemblage of government troops, dogs, automatic weapons, and armored tanks. Linda gets at what the standoff meant to AIM. The last stanza reads,

> No more freeloading on the legends
> of Red Cloud, Crazy Horse, or Big Foot,
> no more borrowed eagle feathers.
> We made our own legends;
> it wasn't easy.

Linda takes us from a one-page monolog in which we first meet Annie to a poem on the next page that sets the larger scene at Wounded Knee and reminds us of the Sioux legacy of courage with no mention of Annie or Mary. On the following page Linda places this poem:

> I miss Annie's hands
> Tucking a few troublesome strands of black hair
> Back behind her ears.
>
> I miss the small gestures in mid-air
> Like wings of sparrows
> Flying up to punctuate the telling
> Of the short sad story of her life.
>
> I think about Annie's hands, small brown fingers
> That stroked my forehead
> And endured my crushing grip in labor pain at Wounded Knee
>
> I shudder at Annie's hands
> Gripping the cold handle of a Colt .45
> She carried to protect herself
> Against government goons:
> Small hands
> Waving away caution
> Even in the face of death.
>
> I remember Annie's hands
> Wiping my tears, then
> holding me in embrace
> When I saw her for the last time.
>
> I miss Annie's hands.

FROM THE *TIMES NEWS*, CRAWFORD, NE, MARCH 16, 1975:

Wanblee, Pine Ridge Reservation. Local FBI agents are investigating the death of an unidentified Indian female found Friday near Wanblee. Agents believe the body may be that of Annie Mae Aquash missing since November of last year. Aquash has been sought in connection with underground activities related to the American Indian Movement. The body has been sent to Scotts Bluff for autopsy to determine cause of death. Physical evidence has been sent to the FBI crime lab for analysis.

Following this is an objective, third-person narrative of a page and a half, the longest single genre in Linda's paper. The narrative tells of the exhumation of an unmarked grave. The characters are a sheriff with a court exhumation order, a state pathologist, a cemetery official, and a middle-aged American Indian. I'll excerpt from the narrative at the moment the coffin is raised from the grave and deposited on the ground:

The three officials stepped forward without hesitation; the Indian stood still for a moment as if his legs wouldn't move, then finally stepped forward to a place at the foot of the casket. The pathologist inserted the key to unlock the lid and turned it once; the top lifted open a little, and he pushed the lid further back to allow an unobstructed view.

"It won't look very good; the body was unclaimed and they don't do much to fix them up." Pulling back the sheet that covered the body just enough to expose the face, he said, "You can see how the side of the face is flattened because the body laid face down through the winter before the FBI found it. Mr. Nogeeshik, would you step forward, please, sir, and identify the body; then I can have the sheriff here transport it to the coroner's office for my investigation."

The Indian moved forward uncertainly to the side of the casket where the pathologist stood. He turned his eyes reluctantly to her face and nodded slightly. "That's her," he said. Nogeeshik's eyes lingered on the sheet covering the body. Unexpectedly, he reached into the casket and pulled the sheet down, exposing the arms and torso. Even from where they were standing, the men could see discolorations across the abdomen, evidence of severe bruising, but Nogeeshik's attention was focused on something entirely different. "Her hands," he said choking, "her hands . . . ," and he took a staggering step backward looking away, into the wind. The three officials surged forward . . . craning their necks to see what the Indian had seen.

"My god," cursed the pathologist. "Those sons of bitches."

"Geez, why would they cut off her hands—and then just throw them in there like that? What's the matter with those stupid bastards?" the sheriff asked, staring in disbelief at the severed hands thrown carelessly alongside the body.

"Expediency, sheriff; expediency. The FBI has built its reputation on it. See the inked fingertips? The body had to be autopsied here; the fingerprinting needed to be done in D.C.—so. It all makes a bizarre kind of sense."

Focusing on this unnerving discovery, none of the men had noticed the Indian's leaving until they turned to speak to him and he was gone.

"Can't blame the poor bastard for clearing out," the cemetery official said. "Most dogs get a more decent burial than this."

When I read Linda's paper and encountered that startling detail of Annie's mutilated corpse—after first getting to know Annie and reading the poem of her strong, soothing hands and then glossing over the final, throwaway detail of the news story, which mentions physical evidence sent to the FBI—after all that, I was knocked back on my reader-response heels. I was informed all right. But I was moved, too, deeply so. The combination of meaning, recurring image, and craft is what did it to me.

Early in their multigenre work, immerse your students in a number of examples of repetition, repetend, and recurring image. Use multigenre papers and/or examples from literature and film. (This concept can be shown dramatically with videos.) Discuss with students what writers and directors gain by using such devices. Ask students to find or invent words, phrases, sentences, or images they could repeat in their papers. If students have already begun to generate genres, have them read through their writing and circle language and images that might serve as strong repetitions.

24 | EVALUATION AND GRADING

One persistent problem teachers mention regards the evaluation and grading of multigenre papers. David Klooster asks:

> How do we establish workable and fair evaluation criteria for multigenre papers? Don't the evaluative criteria have to fit this new form as clearly as possible? And if each student will be doing something different from all the others, don't the criteria have to be tailored to each project?

Evaluation and grading of writing are often topics that teachers agonize over. With multigenre papers the topic gets particularly sticky. The "C" word crops up. How do we assess creativity? (Book publishers and agents, I should note, have little trouble doing this. A young adult novel I've written has been rejected thirty-five times.)

Many multigenre teachers have communicated to me about evaluation and grading. These teachers—many of whom I know personally—seem venturesome, conscientious, intelligent, creative, and grounded in classroom realities, regardless of whether they teach high school freshmen or college undergraduates. This is what some of them have to say about evaluating and grading multigenre work, addressing in their own way the questions that David Klooster asks:

Becky Hoag reports that she divides students' multigenre projects into five major areas for which students get grades:

- Research-in-Progress
- Writer's Notebook
- Written Presentation
- Artifact Presentation
- Research Journal

She gives students a handout that describes what she is looking for in all categories so they know up front what is expected of them.

Karen Blanchette devised this guide to help her assign grades:

Multigenre Research Paper Grade

5 genres present (minimum)	50 pts /
6–8 typed pages	25 pts /
Content/historical accuracy	100 pts /
Mechanics/presentation	25 pts /
Documentation/Bibliography	50 pts /
TOTAL POSSIBLE	250 PTS / _____

Melinda Putz evaluates multigenre papers using a student-created version of a Likkert Scale in the categories of Content, Organization, Creativity, End Notes, Works Cited, and Mechanics. There is room on the forms she creates for self-evaluation as well as teacher evaluation. Here is one example:

Criterion: Content (specific facts, thorough; complete picture of topic; many genres; choice of genre fits topic)

Self-Evaluation

Not Yet   Not Bad   Ah Hah!

Teacher Evaluation

Not Yet   Not Bad   Ah Hah!

Sometimes Melinda averages the student's Likkert evaluation and her own. She does this when students have had the opportunity to explain why they marked the scale as they did.

Nanci Bush uses a score sheet that shows the areas she will assess and their relative weight. Students receive a copy of this score sheet before they turn in their papers. Nanci notes her grade for each section on the sheet, circling the number that reflects her assessment of that section, then adds written comments. You can see how much she values the multigenre section itself; it's worth 75 percent of the project.

MULTIGENRE PROJECTS
MRS. BUSH

PROLOGUE   5   6   7   8   9   10
    Tells the reader how to read the paper. May be brief (1/4–1/2 page).

MULTIGENRE SECTION   70   84   98   112   126   150
    A thoughtful and thorough collection of no fewer than five genres responding to a single topic and considering the topic from several vantage points.

There may be some premise (e.g., travel itinerary) connecting the whole piece. A repetend may be used to connect the genres as well.

NOTE PAGE   10   12   14   16   18   20

Reflective in nature, it describes the inspiration for each of the pieces in the project. This is also an ideal place to document specific notes from sources. Might also provide explanation of what is fact and what has been created or assumed about the situation.

BIBLIOGRAPHY   10   12   14   16   18   20

Accurately documents all sources using MLA style.

COMMENTS

Half the page is available for Nanci's written comments. She is still reflecting on the form, still trying to match her evaluation to her instruction. She writes:

> This sheet did not meet my needs completely. Next year I will make it more specific, including higher-level thinking and literary devices to be consistent with our curriculum. I intend to ask students for input on the scoresheet.
>
> The majority of my students received A's. There were some B's and C's; B's were generally earned by students whose papers were a little lacking and did not contain a repetend or premise to connect them. (I really watched for this as I read. I thought it was a feature that evidenced higher-level thinking skills, which are stressed at our school.)

Bill Babine and Jill Pinard of John Stark Regional High School in Weare, New Hampshire, involve juniors in a comprehensive multigenre project as part of their American literature and culture curriculum. Students are required to use six specific genres: poem, collage, illustration, letter, two analytical essays, and a preface. To round out the project, then, students have some choice. They create two more pieces from a list of nine possibilities: song, play, video production, newspaper writing, letter, short story, essay, poetry, a character's scrapbook. During the process of writing their papers, students are given rubrics the teachers have developed for each genre so they are aware of the grading criteria during their work. For example, the rubric for an analytical essay in which students explain how a novel they have read independently reflects the culture and/or history of its setting looks like this:

1 Introductory paragraph: grabber, lead-in, thesis statement   10
2 Organization (topic sentence, clincher, paragraphing)   10
3 Style: word choice and sentence clarity   10
4 Conclusion   10

5 Internal citations and works cited (3 sources and novel)	10
6 Quality of evidence and understanding about the novel plot and/or characters in the historical/cultural setting	50

Bill and Jill have considered a number of factors in establishing their grading criteria: the quality of work they know from experience that students can produce, gaps in students' learning that need to be addressed, the demands of their curriculum, the expectations of their districts, their own aesthetic values and knowledge of writing.

STEPPING BACK FROM RANKING

At the NCTE fall convention in 1998, Henry Giroux delivered a rousing and passionate keynote address about the plight of children in our society. He couldn't talk about children without also talking about teachers, particularly the disrespect afforded them by politicians and corporate America. He told a story of a textbook salesman who showed up at his office door one day hawking "teacher-proof materials."

"Come right in," said Giroux.

The salesman will, no doubt, never forget his harrowing experience in the office of Henry Giroux, an articulate, critical, tireless voice for teacher and student empowerment.

Sometimes I think we teachers seek a similar "teacher-proofness" when we evaluate and grade the work of students. We want to be rigorous; we want to be accountable; and, maybe most important, we want to be fair. We don't want our blindspots to skew our grading. Save me from myself, we seem to say. Let me clearly evaluate what students have done. Let me not err in the opposite way, either, by rewarding students merely because I like them.

Most nobly we seek consistent evaluation techniques for this messy, idiosyncratic business of writing. Somehow—perhaps by breaking down the various parts of writing and assessing them separately, perhaps by grading holistically, perhaps by creating separate grades for content and mechanics—may I objectively measure a student's work so that I can make unbiased, irrefutable decisions about its quality. May I arrive at conclusive absolutes that no one can dispute—not students, not parents, not colleagues, not school board members, not the oracle at Delphi. As can be seen from the various rubrics that multigenre teachers have devised, we can get closer to that elusive fairness.

Only *closer,* though. We never entirely escape our own subjectivity. That's why I seek to make my own subjectivity as informed as possible.

WHAT OF THE STUDENT?

The most embarrassed I ever feel as a teacher occurs after I have determined grades and then discover something that changes my perception of a student's accomplishment. Sometimes it is an assignment or revision I have missed. Sometimes I learn about a students' processes that broadens my view or enriches the context in which that student worked. A lot more was going on than I realized.

By seeking students' perceptions before my evaluation of their work, I try to avoid those post-grading revelations. I often employ portfolios (Romano 1997) in my classes to help me understand my students' learning that might not be apparent from tests, papers, and good faith participation. But when multigenre papers are due—with students usually working right down to the wire—I don't burden them with the further requirement of a portfolio. I do, however, ask students to write reflections to accompany their paper. Coupled with whatever kind of assessment you use to determine the quality of students' work, I urge you to also have students include a personal reflection about that work. It will particularize your evaluation, make you privy to students' behind-the-scenes thinking, attitudes, and processes that will further your understanding of their work. These reflections usually teach me things I cannot otherwise know.

During fifteen or twenty minutes of the class on the day that multigenre papers are due, I ask students to write a memo to accompany their paper that informs me of invisibilities in their work. On different occasions I've chosen four or five of the following queries to ask multigenre writers:

- What surprised you?
- Speak freely about any aspect of doing this paper you'd like advice on.
- What did you learn about writing in different genres as a way of inquiring into your topic and communicating what you know?
- Tell me about the best piece of writing in your paper and describe why it is best.
- Tell me about the weakest piece of writing in your paper and describe why it is weakest.
- What did the multigenre format enable you to do with your topic?
- What was hard about writing your multigenre paper?
- What could have made writing this paper easier?
- What did you learn about content and/or form?

When students answer queries such as these—which I then read before evaluating their papers—I get closer to honoring one of my fundamental beliefs about learning: Human beings grow and develop intellectually. If any place outside the home should make sure that the human experience is enhanced so that chances for growth and development are optimal, school is that place. Approximation needs to be recognized and applauded. *Close* counts for a great deal when people are learning new things and taking risks. Semi-successes and stumbles today pave the way for successes tomorrow. I am proud, for example, of the first poem I wrote on my own when I was eighteen years old amid the painful downward spiral of lost love. But I would never write that poem today—the rhyming was ludicrous and extreme, the rhythm methodical and lugubrious. But writing that poem was incalculably important to me both psychologically and as a writer trying to grow. When I consider my development since then, I'm amazed. If you evaluate the poem solely on its literary accomplishment without considering my literacy development at that time, it doesn't receive a high mark. Disregarding development and context when evaluating is asking for miseducation, is asking for students to become bitter and alienated, is asking for them to be tyrannized and demeaned by the judgments of others.

For all my concern with quality and accountability, I must keep in mind that I am not as concerned with where students are today as I am with where they could be tomorrow. So I try to work in good faith with all students in my classes, those destined to write throughout the years ahead and those who will never again compose so many words in a fifteen-week stretch. Jim Mims, a writing teacher at the University of Minnesota at Morris, touches this subject when he writes about the major benefit he finds in the multi-genre paper:

> One thing I know is that the majority of students enjoy the multi-genre paper, do reasonable work, and I like it because I have a chance to ensure they get some sense of pleasure and accomplishment from what may be their final writing class at UMM.

I must work in good faith with the young woman whose language skills and analytical ability exceed mine, who writes with candor and eloquence and triumph about her life, and I must work in equally good faith with the young man who tells me he would rather write a formal term paper than reveal himself in writing, who struggles to get words on the page and, when he succeeds in doing so, leans toward fragmented abstractions.

In the end when we evaluate student work, we are left with who we are, the culture we're trying to maintain in our classroom, our own history as writers, institutional pressures, and the undeniable fact of each student's individuality. We communicate to students what a multigenre paper might look like, how it might be constructed, what some of its features could be. We work with students during their processes of writing—perhaps grading weekly pieces as Sirpa Grierson does or requiring that two genres be turned in every two weeks as another teacher does, conferring individually with students several times during the writing as I do. We offer students strategies and genres to try. We have students share the gold of their imaginations in class—and the instructive dross as well. We work hard to create a classroom synergy that makes creativity boil and bubble.

And I can't grade students' multigenre papers without considering—in addition to their accomplishment—their present development, their degree of good faith effort, and the learning culture of my classroom.

EPILOG
TAKING THE PLUNGE

I heard of the multigenre paper in the summer of 1993, but it really took several encounters with it before I was confident enough to try it. I read Writing with Passion *in early 1997. I saw Tom speak twice. After seeing more samples of multigenre papers—especially after a "group reading" of one student's paper— in the Spring of 1998 I was ready to take the leap.*

Nanci Bush, Solon High School

In October 1995, *Language Arts* published a poem I'd sent to editor Bill Teale. One manuscript reviewer, I found out, thought that teachers would resonate to the poem's topic and spirit. I'd thought so, too.

Teaching

Like inching out
on the highboard on buckling knees
when you're seven years old . . .

Paralysis locks your unswallowing throat.
Fear coils and tightens 'round your chest.

At the edge you stand, rigid,
leaning away, holding back.

Possibility seethes beneath you.
Your head bends and body falls.

You plunge into teaching,
suddenly immersed in students,
aswim in writing, reading, talk.

In slow motion you move
through the quickening day
'til you push off the bottom
at three-thirty and burst into sunshine.

You do not gasp.
Your lungs are filled with learning.

171

A month after publication I received a thick manila envelope in the mail from Jill Ostrow, an elementary school teacher in Portland, Oregon, author of *A Room with a Different View* (1995). I'd met Jill a year earlier at an NCTE conference. The envelope contained a brief note from her:

> Tom, I loved your poem so much in *Language Arts* that I brought it to school yesterday and read it to my kids. They also loved it and they decided to draw you some illustrations of what they thought of when they heard it. I loved these so much! I just knew you had to see them. Remember, my kids are much younger than your students— 6, 7, 8, and 9 year olds! But I bet your students will get a kick out of seeing the illustrations.

The one who got the biggest kick out of the illustrations was me. Some were watercolors, some crayon, some pen or pencil. I still love looking at these illustrations and sharing them with students and teachers. And not because the children's work is cute. Cute is ephemeral, shallow, and often— perhaps unintentionally—dismissive. Cute doesn't begin to describe the thinking, humanity, and humor that Jill's students revealed through their illustrations. The children were confident learners, eager to express and share their perceptions.

Their illustrations expanded my vision of teaching and learning. One child rendered the diving board in multiple images to show its springiness. The board looked unstable and flimsy, just like the start that many of us had in the teaching profession. Below the diving teacher is a frowning student. This reminded me how some students would rather suffer tetanus shots than attend school. Another of Jill's students seemed to have the right brain–left brain phenomenon figured out. Her swimming pool featured letters on one side, numbers on the other, and a thick brown line down the middle, the corpus callosum, I guess. Another illustration depicted a figure bent nearly double, twisting and diving toward a steaming cup of coffee. Yes, I thought, I have engaged in such gyrations myself as I juggled subject matter, students, parents, colleagues, mandated testing, and occasional adversarial administrators.

Amid my passion for seeing and saying with words, Jill and her students remind me that changing the mode of expression adds richness and complexity to thinking, catapults us and our audience into other ways of knowing.

I revel in seeing human minds at work. There is no right or wrong about this. It is simply remarkable to see people make meaning, regardless of their age and the meaning they make. We teachers—if we are paying attention to those whom we teach and expecting more of them than rudimentary thinking and memorization—see this common miracle of sense making all the time. No wonder we take the plunge. And Mary, bless her, reminds me that the most significant learning comes when students launch their own dives and teach the teacher.

APPENDIX
MULTIGENRE TEACHERS

These teachers helped me think about multigenre papers and, in many cases, sent me their teaching ideas and students' work. I have quoted many of these teachers in the book. All of them have given me permission to publish their names and institutional and e-mail addresses so that readers might get in touch with them for further information about their work with multigenre papers.

Camille Allen
Education Department
Salve Regina University
Newport, RI 02840
allenc@salve5.salve.edu
College Students

Sue Amendt
Indiana Area High School
450 North Fifth St.
Indiana, PA 15701
samendt@yourinter.net
Grade 11

Bill Babine
John Stark Regional High School
618 North Stark Hwy.
Weare, NH 03281
bilbine@aol.com
Grades 9–12

Brittany Ballard
Mount Notre Dame High School
711 East Columbia Ave.
Cincinnati, OH 45215
bballard@rocketmail.com
Grades 9, 11, 12

Laney Bender Slack
Mason High School
770 Mason-Montgomery Rd.
Mason, OH 45040
slackd@mason.k12.oh.us
Grades 11–12

Karen Blanchette
University of Central Florida
College of Education/Instructional Programs
Orlando, FL 32816
kablanch@bellsouth.net
Grades 9–11

Nanci Bush
Solon High School
33600 Inwood Dr.
Solon, OH 44139
nmbush@sprintmail.com
Grades 9, 11

Cathy Malone Cook
T. Badin High School
571 New London Rd.
Hamilton, OH 45013
ccook@stephen-t-badin.cnd.pvt.k12.oh.us
Grades 9–10

Alys Culhane
English Department
MSC #40
Plymouth State College
Plymouth, NH 03264
aculhane@oz.plymouth.edu
College

Renee Dickson
Princeton High School
11080 Chester Rd.
Sharonville, OH 45246
rjwing@prodigy.net
Grades 10–12

Mary Fuller
Department of English
Miami University
Oxford, OH 45056
Fullermj@muohio.edu
First-year and advanced composition

John Gaughan
Lockland High School
249 West Forrer Ave.
Lockland, OH 45215
john.gaughan@prodigy.net
Grades 9–12

Sirpa Grierson
Brigham Young University
3117 JKHB
PO Box 26245
Provo, UT 84602-6245
sirpa_grierson@byu.edu
College and K–12 public schools

Jill C. Heffner
Western Row Elementary
755 Western Row Rd.
Mason, OH 45040
heffnerj@mason.k12.oh.us
Grade 4

Becky Hoag
Tom C. Clark High School
Northside ISD
5150 DeZavala Rd.
San Antonio, TX 78249
BEHoag@aol.com
Grade 9 Honors

Kathleen Knight Abowitz
Department of Educational Leadership
350 McGuffey Hall
Miami University
Oxford, OH 45056
knightk2@po.muohio.edu
College students

Chris Krueger
Green Bay Southwest High School
1331 Packerland Dr.
Green Bay, WI 54304
ckrueger@netnet.net
Grades 10–11

Dorelle Malucci
Indian Hill High School
6855 Drake Rd.
Cincinnati, OH 45243
maluccid@ih.k12.oh.us
Grade 10

Linda Miller-Cleary
417 Humanities
University of Minnesota, Duluth
Duluth, MN 55812
lmillerc@d.umn.edu
College

Jim Mims
University of Minnesota-Morris
600 East 4th St.
Morris, MN 56267
mimsjj@mrs.umn.edu
College, entry level

Stephanie Musselman
Loveland Hurst Middle School
801 S. Lebanon Rd.
Loveland, OH 45140
MusselSt@loveland.k12.oh.us
Grade 8

Kris Naftel
Kalamazoo Central High School
2432 North Drake Rd.
Kalamazoo, MI 49006
Grades 9–12

Sandy Nesvig
Annunciation School
525 West 54th St.
Minneapolis, MN 55419
sandy.nesvig@annunciationmsp.org
Grades 7–8

Vivian Nida
Putnam City North High School
11800 North Rockwell Ave.
Oklahoma City, OK 73162
gnida@earthlink.net
Grades 10–12

Jill Pinard
John Stark Regional High School
618 North Stark Hwy.
Weare, NH 03281
jill@absomagic.com
Grade 11

Melinda Putz
Ithaca High School
710 North Union St.
Ithaca, MI 48847
mputz@remcen.ehhs.emich.edu
Grades 9–12

Mary Rollinger
Maple Grove Junior-Senior High School
Dutch Hollow Rd.
Bemus Point, NY 14712
mer@cecomet.net
Grade 11, English Regents
Grade 12, Advanced Placement

Cindy Sabik
Gilmour Academy Upper School
34001 Cedar Rd.
Gates Mills, OH 44040
sabikc@ameritech.net

Jennifer Sauvey
Wyoming Middle School
17 Wyoming Ave.
Wyoming, OH 45215
JLS1121@aol.com
Grades 7–8

Vicki Scott
623 Water St.
Batesville, AR 72501
wldwoman@ipa.net
Writing/Arts in Education Consultant

Yvonne Slusser
Western Row School
755 Western Row Rd.
Mason, OH 45040
slussery@mason.k12.oh.us
Grade 3

Georgia Swing
The Marshall School
1215 Rice Lake Rd.
Duluth, MN 55811
Gswing@marshallschool.org
Grades 9–12

WORKS CITED

Avi. 1991. *Nothing but the Truth*. New York: Avon.

Ballard, Brittany. 1998. "Face and Gender: Re-Examining the Multi-Genre Project." Master's thesis, Miami University, Oxford, Ohio.

Behn, Robin, and Chase Twitchell, eds. 1992. *The Practice of Poetry: Writing Exercises from Poets Who Teach*. New York: HarperCollins.

Bishop, Wendy, ed. 1997. *Elements of Alternate Style: Essays on Writing and Revision*. Portsmouth, NH: Boynton/Cook.

Boose, Sara. 1999. "Will I 'Run Loose'?" *Voices from the Middle* 6 (March): 18–22.

Brathwaite, Edward Kamau. 1986. *Jah Music*. Mona, Kingston 7, Jamaica: Savacou Cooperative.

Britton, James. 1993. *Language and Learning*. 2d ed. Portsmouth, NH: Boynton/Cook. 1970. Original edition, London: Allen Lane, The Penguin Press.

Bruner, Jerome. 1986. *Actual Minds, Possible Worlds*. Cambridge, MA: Harvard University Press.

Burroway, Janet. 1987. *Writing Fiction: A Guide to Narrative Craft*. 2d ed. Glenview, IL: Scott, Foresman.

Butler, Octavia. 1979. *Kindred*. Boston: Beacon Press.

Caldwell, Gail. 1994. "Ondaatje's Odyssey." *Boston Globe*, 18 February, 41.

Chieftains, The. 1992. *The Best of the Chieftains*. Sony Music Entertainment, Inc.

Coman, Carolyn. 1995. *What Jamie Saw*. New York: Penguin.

Crow Dog, Mary, with Richard Erdoes. 1990. *Lakota Woman*. New York: HarperCollins.

Crutcher, Chris. 1995. *Ironman*. New York: Greenwillow.

Didion, Joan. 1979. *The White Album*. New York: Pocket Books.

Draper, Sharon. 1994. *Tears of a Tiger*. New York: Atheneum.

Dubus, Andre. 1991. *Broken Vessels*. Boston: David R. Godine.

Elbow, Peter. 1990. *What Is English?* Urbana, IL: NCTE.

Emig, Janet. 1972. *The Composing Processes of Twelfth Graders.* Urbana, IL: NCTE.

Fleischman, Paul. 1988. *Joyful Noise: Poems for Two Voices.* New York: HarperTrophy.

Fletcher, Ralph. 1996. *Breathing In, Breathing Out: Keeping a Writer's Notebook.* Portsmouth, NH: Heinemann.

Fu, Danling. 1995. *My Trouble Is My English.* Portsmouth, NH: Heinemann.

Garrett, Pat. 1980. *The Authentic Life of Billy, the Kid.* Time-Life Books. Original edition, 1882. Santa Fe, NM: New Mexican Print and Publishing Co.

Gaughan, John. 1998. "From Comfort Zone to Contact Zone." *English Journal* 87 (February): 36–43.

Grossman, Florence. 1982. *Getting From Here to There: Writing and Reading Poetry.* Montclair, NJ: Boynton/Cook.

Hass, Robert, ed. and trans. 1994. *The Essential Haiku: Versions of Bashō, Buson, and Issa.* Hopewell, NJ: The Ecco Press.

Heard, Georgia. 1995. *Writing Toward Home: Tales and Lessons to Find Your Way.* Portsmouth, NH: Heinemann.

———. 1989. *For the Good of the Earth and Sun: Teaching Poetry.* Portsmouth, NH: Heinemann.

Hughes, Langston. 1996. *The Collected Poems of Langston Hughes.* New York: Alfred A. Knopf.

Janeczko, Paul, ed. 1983. *Poetspeak: In Their Work, About Their Work.* New York: Collier.

Johnson, David. 1990. *Word Weaving.* Urbana, IL: NCTE.

Kingsolver, Barbara. 1995. *High Tide in Tucson: Essays from Now or Never.* New York: HarperCollins.

Kirk, Rahsaan Roland. 1973. *Bright Moments.* Atlantic Recording Corporation.

Lamott, Anne. 1994. *Bird By Bird: Some Instructions on Writing and Life.* New York: Pantheon Books.

Macauley, Robie, and George Lanning. 1987. *Technique in Fiction, Second Edition: Revised and Updated for a New Generation.* New York: St. Martin's Press.

McCracken, Nancy Mellen. 1992. "Gender Issues and the Teaching of Writing." In *Gender Issues in the Teaching of English*, edited by Nancy Mellen McCracken and Bruce Appleby. Portsmouth, NH: Boynton/Cook.

McKnight, Brian. 1995. "The Long and Wonderful Odyssey of the Walrus: A Heart Play." In *Writing with Passion* by Tom Romano. Portsmouth, NH: Boynton/Cook.

Michaels, Judith Rowe. 1999. *Risking Intensity: Reading and Writing Poetry with High School Students.* Urbana, IL: NCTE.

Mr. Holland's Opus. 1995. Directed by Stephen Herek. Writing credit: Patrick Duncan. Buena Vista Pictures.

Moyers, Bill. 1995. *Poetry: The Language of Life*. Fourth program of an eight-part series with Bill Moyers. New Bridge Communications. Originally shown on PBS, 1995. 58 minutes.

Murray, Donald M. 1996. *Crafting a Life in Essay, Story, Poem*. Portsmouth, NH: Boynton/Cook.

———. 1993. *Write to Learn*. 4th ed. New York: Harcourt.

———. 1978. "Internal Revision: A Process of Discovery." In *Research on Composing: Points of Departure,* edited by Charles R. Cooper and Lee Odell. Urbana, IL: NCTE.

Newkirk, Thomas. 1997. *The Performance of Self in Student Writing*. Portsmouth, NH: Boynton/Cook.

Night and Fog. 1955. Directed by Alain Resnais. Writing credit: Jean Cayrol.

Oliver, Mary. 1994. *A Poetry Handbook*. New York: Harcourt Brace.

Ondaatje, Michael. 1984. *The Collected Works of Billy the Kid*. New York: Penguin. 1970. Original edition, Toronto: House of Anansi Press.

———. 1976. *Coming Through Slaughter*. Toronto, Canada: General Publishing Co. Ltd.

Ostrow, Jill. 1995. *A Room with a Different View*. York, ME: Stenhouse.

Romano, Tom. 1997. "Portfolio on Portfolios." *English Education* 29 (3): 158–72.

———. 1995a. *Writing with Passion: Life Stories, Multiple Genres*. Portsmouth, NH: Boynton/Cook.

———. 1995b. "Teaching." *Language Arts* 72 (16): 415.

———. 1994. "Removing the Blindfold: Portfolios in Fiction Writing Classes." In *New Directions In Portfolio Assessment: Reflective Practice, Critical Theory, and Large-Scale Scoring,* edited by Laurel Black, Donald A. Daiker, Jeffrey Sommers, and Gail Stygall. Portsmouth, NH: Boynton/Cook.

———. 1987. *Clearing the Way: Working with Teenage Writers*. Portsmouth, NH: Heinemann.

Rosenblatt, Louise. 1978. *The Reader, the Text, the Poem: The Transactional Theory of Reader Response*. Carbondale, IL: Southern Illinois University Press.

Schindler's List. 1993. Directed by Steven Spielberg. United International Pictures.

Shapard, Robert, and James Thomas, eds. 1986. *Sudden Fiction: American Short-Short Stories*. Salt Lake City: Peregrine Smith Books.

Smoke Signals. 1998. Directed by Chris Eyre. Writing credit: Sherman Alexie. Miramax Films.

Stafford, William. 1986. *You Must Revise Your Life*. Ann Arbor: University of Michigan Press.

Stafford, William, and Stephen Dunning. 1992. *Getting the Knack: 20 Poetry Writing Exercises*. Urbana, IL: NCTE.

Thomas, James, Denise Thomas, and Tom Hazuka. 1992. *Flash Fiction: 72 Very Short Stories*. New York: W. W. Norton.

Tsujimoto, Joe. 1988. *Teaching Poetry Writing to Adolescents*. Urbana, IL: NCTE.

Weathers, Winston. 1980. *An Alternate Style: Options in Composition*. Rochelle Park, NJ: Hayden Book Co.

Webster's American Biographies. 1975. Edited by Charles Van Doren. Springfield, MA: G. & C. Merriam Company.

Williams, William Carlos. 1985. *Selected Poems*. New York: New Directions Books.

Witherall, Carol, and Nel Noddings. 1991. *Stories Lives Tell: Narrative and Dialogue in Education*. New York: Teachers College Press.

ACKNOWLEDGMENTS

Writing for me is a slow, fulfilling process. It makes me feel useful in this world. Endorphins, bright moments, significant work, play, invention, creation—optimal psychological experience. I often wish, though, that I had greater conceptual skills in the beginning of a writing project. It would save me much time. What gets my books written is stamina, not brilliance. Process is my friend. Joining process and stamina are many people who work in my corner when I'm writing a book. No them, no book.

I extend my unwavering gratitude to the following:

Miami University granted me a Faculty Research Appointment for Fall 1998. That semester, one full summer before it, and part of the next summer enabled me to get a draft of this book written.

The secretaries in the Department of Teacher Education at Miami University—Kristy Adams, Linda Dennett, and Diane Francis—make my job run smoother. They teach and reteach me routines I should have learned by now.

My department chair, David Killian, filled in teaching gaps caused by my leave and wished me good writing.

These indispensable people helped me locate multigenre teachers and former students: Ken Brewer, Ann Friedli, Dick Harmston, Tim King, Julie Lewis, Phyllis Neumann, Tom Newkirk, Jill Ostrow, and many parents.

Former students, current teachers—Jen Sauvey and Angie Bellia—bought me *The Essential Haiku* by Robert Hass on the occasion of *their* graduation and so are directly responsible for the haiku section in "The Many Ways of Poems."

My students these past nine years at Miami and Utah State University have shown me so many multigenre possibilities. Their work is what inspired this book.

Many teachers from around the country communicated with me about their multigenre projects with students. They have been indispensable to my thinking and teaching. Their names and addresses are gratefully listed in the Appendix.

I especially thank teachers, administrators, and students of the Mason City Schools in Ohio, three of which are partner schools associated with the Institute for Educational Renewal based at Miami University. Superintendent Kevin Bright asked me to teach my graduate class in teaching writing on site at Mason. That work has been a professional and personal boon for me. I hope the teachers I've worked with have experienced some of the renewal and growth that I have from learning with them, visiting their classrooms, and writing with their students.

Tom Newkirk keeps inviting me to the University of New Hampshire to work with teachers in the summer, and Don Murray casually and consistently reminds me that I am a writer.

Susan Stires, my sometime summer teaching partner at UNH, is ever sensitive to language. She helped me get one small, crucial part of this book right.

Sally Joranko at John Carroll University invited me to campus to work with high school students, their faculty, and her colleagues in a stimulating, exploratory, upbeat atmosphere.

Max Morenberg of Miami is a linguist, grammarian, and word man par excellence. He is all that with Groucho's humor and a knack for finding just about anything on the Internet. My dear Max, we'll always have "Lydia."

Ruth Hubbard and Ralph Fletcher are fine writers, sharp minds, and great souls. They read my prospectus and wrote to me about it. They set high expectations and made me want to write more.

Bill Strong listened to a first draft of my introduction as we sat on a houseboat on Lake Powell in southern Utah. He said, "You're in a different place now." He said, "That first part sounds important to you but doesn't seem to fit." And I came unstuck.

John Gaughan is a teacher, author, and longtime friend. He read early drafts of many of the chapters and responded amid teaching, parenting, writing, coaching, and professional activity.

Brenda Miller Power read my entire, bloated manuscript and wrote me eight, single-spaced pages of pointed response. "Tom," she wrote, "you are not a self-indulgent man."

"Brenda," I said the first time I saw her, "I am a very self-indulgent man." Her critique, composed of suggestions, directives, encouragement, and hard truth, guided me toward a leaner, more helpful, much better book.

Heinemann has been good to me over the last fifteen years and I would like to thank:

Renee Nicholls, my copy editor.

Vicki Kasabian, my production editor.

Judy Arisman, who designed the cover.

Bill Varner, my editor, worked with me through incipient thinking, exploration, early drafts, even loss, death, grief, and birth. Carpe diem, Bill.

My aunt, Mary Recchio Romano, helped me learn particulars about her mother, Antonia Recchio, who once used garlic and prayers to cure me of sickness when I was a child.

My sister, Nancy McDonald, has loved me longer than anyone. She gave me *Tuesdays with Morrie* at just the right time. She is a golden soul. She, her children, and grandchildren have enriched my life.

Two women: Kathy—wife, lover, and friend—and Mariana—daughter, historian, and teacher—have made life sweet, safe, and sometimes tempestuous. I couldn't do this journey without them.

My Mom, Mae Romano Carnahan, passed away five days after I sent the final manuscript of this book to Heinemann. For fifty years she was a continual brightness in my life, so much good humor and equanimity did she embody. She was a tall woman who stood five feet two.

When I visited Mom in the weeks before her death, I sat at her bedside, sometimes reading a Sue Grafton mystery to her, sometimes helping her eat food we made: chicken with garlic, mashed potatoes and gravy, creamed chicken with biscuits. The last time I sat with her she urged me to go home. "You won't finish your book," she said. "I'll finish it," I answered and stayed with her a little longer. Not long enough, though. Not long enough. I so wish she were here.

There is this, however: When my last visit ended, Mom and I kissed and said good-bye. I reminded her of the day I would come again. A few minutes later as I stood at the elevator, an impulse shot through me. I turned and walked back to her room. When I stepped inside, she looked up at me, surprised at my appearance, expectant of some explanation.

"I just wanted to see your face one more time," I said.

Mom's quick smile lit the room, and then she spoke the last word I would hear her say.

She said, "Good."

CREDITS